T0336440

PERSEVERANCE

Broke to Billions

PERSEVERANCE

Broke to Billions

*Barriers in Business
and Strategies
to Remove Them*

Chuck Whittall

Post Hill
PRESS

A POST HILL PRESS BOOK

Perseverance: Broke to Billions:
Barriers in Business and Strategies to Remove Them
© 2020 by Chuck Whittall
All Rights Reserved

ISBN: 978-1-64293-661-2
ISBN (eBook): 978-1-64293-662-9

Cover design by Alyssa Curry
Interior design and composition by Greg Johnson, Textbook Perfect

This is a work of nonfiction. All people, locations, events, and situations are portrayed to the best of the author's memory.

Post Hill Press
New York • Nashville
posthillpress.com
Published in the United States of America
1 2 3 4 5 6 7 8 9 0

We should want to pass along what we know, provide opportunities for those seeking them, and lift others to see over walls to view the vast opportunities they may not have otherwise been aware existed.

—CHUCK WHITTALL

To you, the reader, who will go the extra mile in life.

To the individual who didn't grow up privileged but realizes there is no barrier you can't get through regardless of your background.

To those who have been bullied and risen above with the unstoppable desire to succeed.

To people who have been told they can't but do.

To the optimistic individuals who would throw a life preserver rather than a bucket of water to one who is drowning.

To those who give back to others and can see the greater good.

To the fighters—those individuals who truly don't give up but choose to persevere.

I have relentlessly, with all my heart and soul, persevered my entire life through everything I have done. This book is for all those who have or will now make the choice to persevere.

Contents

Foreword

In life there are visionaries and vision makers. Visionaries are a dime a dozen. They see possibilities and do nothing. Opportunity slips by, over and over again. They just can't pull the trigger for a variety of reasons. The real reason is always fear.

The vision makers are few and far between. Oh yes, they are fearful, but their instincts and belief in themselves allow them to go forward. To be bold. To dream and then do. Visionaries are dreamers. Vision makers are doers.

Chuck Whittall is a vision maker extraordinaire. The impossible to most is possible to him. Fear is not an emotion that fills him. He is not reckless or erratic, but determined and thoughtful. When most people see obstacles, he sees a back door, a tunnel, or comes in by helicopter. The most desirable projects become his because he finds a way. Like magic tricks, they all seem simple once you know how they're done.

I invest with Chuck because I have seen his magic over and over again. I think of myself as a vision maker, and I admire them. I know how hard it is to say yes when all the smart people are saying no.

His reputation is impeccable. Our town is a small circle. Bad reputations are well known. Chuck is known as an honest doer who does what he says. Over time that reputation becomes one's legacy.

Chuck is a dreamer *and* a doer. He is the one who says yes when most say no. He is the rare visionary who then becomes the vision maker. I can't wait to learn about his latest vision. And if he is kind enough, I would like to invest. I own race horses and spend lots of time at tracks. But when I bet, I rarely bet on the horse. I always bet on the jockey. If Chuck is riding, I don't care what horse he is on. I'm betting on him.

—*John Morgan*
   "Faith Without Works Is Dead"

Introduction

I've always known I was meant to do something significant with my life. I had to do the work and define who I was before I knew in what capacity. Although I didn't realize it at the time, kids in school called me poor, which made it uncomfortable just being there. I was often bullied and beat up because of their perspective of me. I didn't feel I carried myself any differently than the other kids, so I didn't understand why I was viewed that way. From that point on, I was determined to figure out a way to stop kids from making fun of me for being underprivileged. I couldn't control the way people felt about me, and that was okay, but if there were a way to change my circumstances, I would be relentless in finding it because it didn't feel good being perceived that way.

As a kid, my vision was limited to what was around me, but I found ways to nurture my creativity. I took the initiative to climb the proverbial wall and see what was on the other side. I'm not implying that what I saw was more comfortable or better—but there was more real estate, which equated to further opportunities. Once I realized what existed beyond the limitations of my environment, my desire to set and achieve bigger goals led me in the direction of my destiny, and there was no end—because the world is covered in real estate!

That self-realization of believing I was meant to do more derived from being present throughout my journey and paying attention not only to what I needed, but also to the needs of others. If I wanted to be impactful, whatever I did had to be effective enough to be life-changing and lasting. So I began. It wasn't easy, and it didn't happen quickly, because I had to be a good student, committed to the work that needed to be done, learn from the experts, and remain optimistic in my approach. But I had to identify *why* I wanted to be successful and *what* success meant to me.

It took years, but what I had access to first was learning how to successfully operate a company through trial and error, and then I learned how to grow it. When my practices and foundation were unyielding, and opportunities were there to fight for, I worked to help the people around me achieve success by showing them how the power of perseverance works. Refusing to quit or give up on something despite difficulties takes discipline, work ethic, patience, and passion. It's never easy, but in the long run, it's worth it, and it will definitely knock out some of the competition. In short, having perseverance created my financial independence. How? I fought hard.

My past left me with the most inspiring and disheartening memories. We all have them. It's what we do with those recollections that shapes our outlook and determines our future. That's why I reflect on the experiences I've had during various stages of my life. I recall people I've met along the way and obstacles I was forced to overcome. Those encounters are what caused me to make decisions that kept me pursuing the path I traveled—and in time, it all made sense.

There were occasions when my decisions didn't bring what I expected to fruition. However, as though divinely created, I knew that path was mine. It was up to me to go the distance despite the barriers I was sure to stumble upon, and I had plenty. I still have them. The difference is, I don't possess a negative way of thinking; I'm an optimist. I put energy toward finding solutions that lead to positive results. If you don't see a solution, create one.

The jobs I've had and businesses I've built were fun, meaningful adventures that caused me to crave more out of life. I didn't want more out of greed; I wanted more because I was confident that I was capable of obtaining it. I paid attention to details and became observant of situations and moments that inspired me to do what I love—and that was build. I didn't want to have a good job and create an income. My objective was to build properties people loved along with a successful career, which would stem from having behaviors that were congruent with my mindset.

When I began this journey, I didn't have any money. I worked for everything. Starting from broke, I invested time in learning how to do things properly while understanding the reasons some things didn't work. In the process, my confidence evolved, and I became resolute in decisions I made about my future. I was determined not to fail at being successful, and developing a strong work ethic at an early age contributed to my success. Working turned out to be the litmus test that helped me realize I would never be content unless I owned my own business. Once I adopted that thought process, it never faded, and I never deviated from the path I chose regardless of hardships or losses. Being a quick study, I took those transferable lessons and moved on. When the time was right, I made a resurgence in the business of real estate armed with a wealth of experience and knowledge. My willingness to persevere through the Great Recession, a devastating global economic downturn, produced the ability to negotiate the deal that led to billions. And the deal that I made is one that you should make, too.

Several occurrences during my formative years prepared and positioned me for my journey as well as the outcome. One way or another, our experiences always do. With a relentless work ethic, time and perseverance, that dirt path led me to where I am now, the CEO of Unicorp National Developments. We are a nation-wide real estate development company that has exceeded $3 billion in construction and continues to grow. Although it wasn't easy, the route to this destination has had a significant economic impact, and we are far from done.

One of the foremost critical aspects of building a successful business is caring about people. Investing in the success of others and constructing a winning team invested in the success of the company should be a seamless process. When you accomplish that, you've done something special. I've discovered that there is no better way to build a business than taking care of your people first because they are family. If you want your family to trust you, display confidence in your decision-making and leadership through hiring competent individuals that you trust and respect. My intent was to inspire every person at Unicorp to instinctively do the same with one another. I take pride in having cultivated that; however, my biggest accomplishment is that the success of Unicorp National Developments has allowed me to enrich the lives of many people around me. I believe that is an unspoken responsibility of being successful.

Although Unicorp is thriving and operating successfully, I still drive around perusing properties. It's instinctive and connects to my unwavering passion and curiosity. If I find some-thing, I determine whether it's economically feasible. A strength that has been invaluable in my business is that I am a visionary. I create value because I can imagine much more density and what the end product will be. When I have an idea for something, I sketch it out by hand—letting my creativity escape onto paper. I can look at something, envision it differently, and interpret what I see to the architects who design it. I see undeveloped properties for what they could be. When I buy real estate, people tell me all the time, "We never saw that," and that's good. My goal is to make memorable properties where people enjoy the quality of them as well as the landscape. Unicorp's track record has made it easier to move forward.

Building wealth is one thing, but being diligent in working to sustain it is another. One incredible deal can make you, and another can wipe everything away if you have not invested in learning how to sustain wealth. After nearly four decades in business, I wouldn't be where I am without having a solid financial acumen. That wasn't always the case, but I learned that it's a critical prerequisite to success.

Over time, and with each business transaction, I've achieved something so substantial that it has changed my life. In this book, I have disclosed a plethora of barriers in business and communicated strategies to remove them. I've explored practices that have contributed to my success along with the perseverance it took to go from broke to billions. My intent is to encourage you to find your path and stay the course of building financial independence regardless of the adversity you are certain to encounter.

At some point, everyone in the world will face adversity—the loss of children, family, and friends; health-related issues; financial challenges; personal struggles; and hardships in business. It's how you choose to deal with it that affects the outcome.

—CHUCK WHITTALL

Chapter 1

The Inspiration

This is life—and as long as you're breathing, there will be situations that can discourage you enough that you'll give up on or quit whatever dream or goals you had. But if you hang in there long enough to make it through another day and begin the next with a stronger and more resilient mindset, you will find that there are significantly more things to be inspired by—so keep going. That inspiration will draw you closer to your intended destination.

———

While my childhood wasn't without adversity or unfavorable incidents, for the most part, I was happy. Like many others, I've faced my share of tough lessons, one of which taught me that I couldn't control anything other than myself. When I began to focus on developing behaviors and a mindset that I could manage, I became more optimistic about life—then optimism became the weapon I used to defeat adversity.

Along with my younger siblings, Timothy and Heather, my older sister Tammy, and my parents, Barbara and Chuck, we lived in a modest three-bedroom, one-bathroom gray house in the small, picturesque community of Winter Park, Florida, a suburb of Orlando. My sisters shared the first bedroom, my little brother and I occupied the second, and our parents had the third. My parents were frugal, and there were things we lacked, but I always thought we had enough. Although we had a washing machine, at that time I didn't know a dryer existed or that we couldn't afford one. Our clothes were hung on the line in the backyard, and a light wind or the sun dried them just fine. When we didn't have hot water, my mother filled large pots and heated them on the stove so we could take a warm bath, and I couldn't tell the difference.

The negative aspects were undoubtedly present, and when I was a kid, they sometimes caused me to respond in nonconstructive ways. With time, I found that it was beneficial to observe and learn from the good things that happened and contribute to the positive aspects of life. Seeing people happy was a good thing, and one thing I was certain of was that I wanted to make people happy.

Although my baby sister, Heather, and I were the closest, I was usually engaged in activities away from home without my brother or sisters. If I wasn't playing kickball in the unkept field near our house or hanging with friends, I was off using my creativity in some other way. Between the ages of six and eight, I'd go out in that field to search for rocks that were dissimilar, and I'd find a nice assortment. Some were perfect to use as paperweights and others had a unique shape. Each of them had little imperfections that made them special. I thought if I washed the dirt off and painted them, they would look even better, and some of the neighbors would buy them. People like things for different reasons, and when I painted designs on them, I kept that in mind. When the rocks were ready to be sold, I stacked them in my red wagon and pulled it door-to-door, selling the small treasures for a quarter and the larger ones for one dollar. I was right. Most of the people commented on the way I painted them and the colors I used. My neighbors told me that the rocks were cute and my idea was creative. Some of the neighbors bought more than one. The positive feedback and support further stimulated my ingenuity. I believe people pay attention to detail, and something as small as a painted rock could mean something to somebody. Material things typically do. I gave one to Mom and a blue one to Dad so they would think of me when I wasn't with them.

Whenever possible, I'd find opportunities to work wherever they were. I stayed busy making pocket money by doing little jobs around the neighborhood when I was ten. I'd go to a neighbor's house, knock on the door, and ask, "Will you pay me twenty dollars to wash all the windows on your house?"

"I don't need my windows washed."

"Well, you have weeds. Can I pull your weeds?" I'd ask, pointing to them.

"I don't need my weeds pulled."

I was a relentless little kid. The only way most of the neighbors got rid of me was by succumbing to my requests and giving me something to do.

"I'll wash your car for twenty dollars," I offered.

"Fine. Do it."

I ended up washing cars, cleaning windows, pulling weeds, and doing whatever I could because I thought everyone had a need for something at their house. Before I knew it, I was doing chores for people all over the neighborhood, but I was still in search of something more.

My school, Brookshire Elementary, bordered an area called the Winter Park chain of lakes, and wealthy people lived in that ring of homes. The eastern part of Winter Park didn't have any lakes and consisted of smaller homes. Our house was in that area.

From the third grade until the sixth grade, school became challenging because kids started bullying me. I didn't fit in with my siblings, and I didn't fit in at school either. Appreciatively, I wore the clothing my parents were able to supply, and I thought I looked fine, but not according to some of the other kids. They picked on me because of the way I dressed and, for some reason, I was just an easy target.

"Why do you wear the same shoes every day, Chuckie? They're stupid and ugly!" a classmate shouted, making sure everyone around him heard.

I glared at him and mumbled, "'Cuz that's all my parents can afford."

I was never hurt or disappointed that my parents could only manage to buy me one pair of shoes each year and not much in the way of clothing. I didn't know I was supposed to have or need more. What hurt was how mean kids were. They didn't know anything about us, but apparently my appearance mattered more to them than who I was.

I thought the kids picked on me to make sure I knew I wasn't accepted. I was usually pushed and shoved down the hallway by other students on my way to class. The laughter and snickering were piercing, echoing throughout my body. My expression made me appear numb to it, but I wasn't. Being treated that way, especially in front of my peers, made me feel isolated in a world that didn't want me, but I was still in it, so I had to make it work—somehow. I remember thinking, *One day, I'm going to be in a position where I can buy any pair of shoes I want.*

Back then, my Buster Brown shoes were all I had. When I got my first pair of white gym shoes, I was grateful my parents bought them. But another kid laughed as he purposely stepped on my feet, smearing his dirty footprint on both of my shoes. The things kids did to me were emotionally draining.

I didn't have a lot of things, and I didn't ask my parents for anything more than what they gave me, but I took pride in and care of what I had. I folded my clothes neatly before placing them in my dresser drawers, and I kept my shoes as clean as I could, but I was made for running, playing, and staying busy outside. As often as I wore my shoes, they didn't last long.

During elementary school, the teasing and bullying became incessant and turned into fights. All the fighting made me understand that the way I looked was never going to be acceptable. Kids continually found things to pick on, and there was a period of time that I didn't think it would ever stop. For one, I had bad acne at an early age, and second, none of the other kids with siblings wore matching outfits to school. My siblings and I did because my mother sat up at night and on weekends and made them. We looked like the von Trapp family from *The Sound of Music* when we got dressed for school. When kids made fun of me because of the way I dressed, it led to more fights, and sometimes I got beat up by the boys who were stronger than I.

Even though I didn't want to be ridiculed, I never went home and told my mother about the fights or complained about the hateful things kids said to me because I was thankful that I had clean clothes to wear. The time and effort my mother put into making our clothing was special to her. Mom loved us, and that was one of the ways she showed it. Despite any perceived disadvantages, I never knew we were without anything until other kids made it their responsibility to let me know.

I had a lot of time to think about the reasons kids treated me the way they did. Finally, I came to the conclusion that bullying was primarily due to a combination of social dominance and cruel kids acting out. I wasn't either.

Things happen to people that have a profound effect on their life. Sometimes they know in that moment and, for others, it comes after a period of reflection. Good or bad, what people say and how they treat you will leave an imprint. I remember what that kid said to me because it was a defining moment in my life. Those are the very moments that can change you, your purpose, and your drive. Don't stop searching for a solution to make things better, because there is one. Those moments can inspire you to accomplish something perhaps you never would have attempted—or take it all away. Either way, the choice is yours. You don't quit life because people dislike or hurt you.

My intolerance forced its way out in the fourth grade the same way fuel escapes a rocket engine—thrusting it forward. Frederick was a kid who assumed the role of the school bully, and one day he fixated on me. I'd dealt with this stocky kid, who was about the same height as I, enacting his perpetual routine of shoving, tripping, and spewing cruelty until I decided he'd given me his last shove. This kid was known for beating smaller kids to a pulp like it was a hobby, but no one ever stopped him. I wasn't afraid of him—I just didn't want to fight.

After our teacher gave us a reading assignment, she stepped out of the classroom halfway through fourth period. Frederick hopped out of his chair and walked up to me while I was still seated at my desk. His fist was balled up, and he confidently boasted loud enough for everyone to hear, "I'm going to beat you up after school!"

I thought the best way to defend myself was by catching Frederick off guard. I didn't have an advocate, so I advocated for myself. I retorted, "Why wait until after school?" I jumped out of my seat with my arm drawn back and socked Frederick as hard as I could. He stumbled backward, hit the ground, and stayed there sprawled out. Our teacher had returned and came up behind me just in time to bear witness.

To that day, that teacher never stopped Frederick from bullying me or anyone else. No one made an attempt to minimize concentric circles in the classroom to make it a healthier, safer, and more productive environment for kids. But the moment I defended myself, the teacher grabbed my arm, yanking me away from Frederick, yelling, "Chuckie! You're going to the principal's office, now!"

A few minutes later, I was sitting outside of the principal's office awaiting my punishment. The door was partially open, and I heard the principal call my mom and reflectively state, "He gets in too many fights. We have to remove him from school. The only way Chuckie can come back is if he gets counseling."

Over time, the only thing those kids had done with their cruelty was fuel my purpose to create a solution. I didn't want to be like them, and fighting to defend myself wasn't helping. I ended up in counseling as the principal mandated; however, the problems I had at school still persisted.

Shortly after that incident, I joined the Boy Scouts. The Boy Scouts worked to my advantage because they taught us how to establish and achieve goals. Before then, I had known what I didn't want, but I hadn't known how to get what I wanted. I hadn't identified any specific ambitions, and the Boy Scouts changed that for me. They set goals, had merit badges for achievements, and allowed me to climb up the ranks, which taught me to do the same in other areas of my life. I already had a strong spirit, but I wanted to feel more confident, and losing the battle against preadolescent acne didn't help.

The way I was treated by other students and the things they said made me feel awkward, but that feeling of being uncomfortable is what drove me to find my comfort level. And when I did, I refused to become complacent. Being stuck in a place that didn't want me wasn't where I wanted to be. Fighting and getting beat up was mentally and physically exhausting. I'd get up in the morning, get dressed, eat breakfast, and then walk three blocks to school with my heart racing and feeling tense as I wondered which class period I'd have to defend myself. I had to find a way to overcome that obstacle or it would continue.

I sat on the sofa and waited for Mom to come in from work one day. Before she had the chance to set her purse down, I blurted out, "Mom, will you take me to Kmart?"

"Now?"

In a pleading tone I replied, "I'd appreciate it."

Mom let out a drawn-out sigh. With her keys and purse in hand, she turned around and opened the front door. "Let's go before I change my mind," she said, ruffling my hair as I rushed past her.

On the ride to Kmart, Mom didn't ask what I needed, but when she followed me to the exercise equipment, her narrowing eyes told me she understood. I spent forty dollars on a set of weights and a bench. As soon as we got home, I set the weights up and started lifting. I didn't know how much weight to add to the barbell, but it didn't matter; I pushed myself. Every day, I lifted weights in our yard for at least an hour. Since I enjoyed working out, and I became much stronger, I joined the weight lifting club at school, which gave me more confidence.

I appreciated being a Boy Scout because it took my mind off what I was dealing with in school and gave me a sense of belonging. I was able to participate and learn without conflict. There was no fighting or bullying. Everyone seemed driven to accomplish goals and do well. I enjoyed being in that type of nurturing environment. Since the Boy Scouts offered an opportunity to advance, I intended to earn each badge. I aimed to excel at every single thing, with the goal to be in the top percentage of Scouts across the country. A few years later, in 1978, I reached the highest rank attainable and became an Eagle Scout at the age of twelve.

Since the inception of the Boy Scouts, only 4 percent of the Scouts have achieved this status, and hardly any by the age twelve. I took pride in being one of them. Gerald Ford, James Lovell, Michael Bloomberg, Louis Freeh, Neil Armstrong, Steven Spielberg, Donald Rumsfeld, H. Ross Perot, Robert Gates, Sam Walton, and J. Willard Marriott were a few of the more prominent Eagle Scouts. Being an Eagle Scout enhanced my values, decision-making, ethics, and personal development. I became more focused on and passionate about the things I did.

———•———

My father was a firefighter, and he served our community well. Other than being his son, we didn't have much of a relationship. He worked during the day and often had night jobs that kept him from being available for my Boy Scout trips or much else. The day he got Tammy and me tickets to the opening week of Walt Disney World in 1971 is etched in my memory. Dad wasn't able to spend the day with us because he had to work at Disney as a firefighter, but Mom stayed with us the entire day. The experience was unbelievable. I'll never forget how much fun I had with my mom and sister. The things Disney created for people to enjoy and their attention to detail were beyond my young imagination. It never left me.

At around eleven years of age, I played soccer and Little League baseball. One Saturday morning, my father grabbed a mitt, came out to the yard, and played catch with me. Although it only happened once, it felt good to have that time with Dad.

As a hobby, I'd sit quietly in my room and put together model cars, airplanes, and helicopters. Over time, I ended up with an impressive collection of them arranged uniformly on my dresser. Although I didn't think it would be an easy feat, they were reminders of what I wanted to have when I grew up. It was a dream—but somehow, I believed it was possible to turn that dream into reality.

One evening when my father was home, he came into my room after dinner to see what I was doing. When I showed him the model kit I was about to work on, he sat down and helped me build the helicopter I had just removed from the box. When we finished, Dad got a string, tied it around the helicopter and proudly hung it over my bed. I cherished those memories, but over time, I extinguished others.

After that, I didn't see my father too often, but a few months later, Dad lightly tapped on my door, opened it, and walked into my bedroom again. I thought maybe he wanted to build another model together. Only this time, Dad appeared a bit uncomfortable. When he spoke, he revealed, "Your mother and I are getting a divorce. I'm moving out." I could only manage to stare at him blankly while he paused long enough for me to respond. I didn't think there was anything I could say to alter his decision, and it wasn't a question, so I didn't reply. It wasn't until that moment that I realized his telling me was nothing more than a formality; Dad had already left us a long time ago. He turned around and vacated the room without saying anything else. Initially, I was hurt, then I became angry. I don't think either of my parents considered the magnitude their decision to divorce would have on us because nothing was discussed, at least not with me. The psychological aspect was a burden for me to figure out or manage on my own, but it was harder than I ever would have imagined it to be—probably because I didn't expect it. After I heard the front door shut, I went into my closet, grabbed my wooden baseball bat, and broke the helicopter into what seemed like a thousand pieces. I collapsed across my bed, sobbing as hard as I ever had. I was getting bullied in school and already having a tough time. Although Dad wasn't home much, I didn't want him to leave forever. But that day was the last time I ever saw him.

Everyone has something that has broken them down or hurt them terribly, and I wondered if I was the only kid to feel that way. When I pulled myself together and finally sat up, I looked at the pieces on the floor and thought, *Every kid has their helicopter.*

———

Camping trips were synonymous with the Boy Scouts, and when we had them, some of the fathers were kind enough to ask, "Chuckie, do you want to come with us?" The environment was inspiring, and it made me happy, so I went. The other fathers didn't necessarily pull me aside and mentor me on those trips, but indirectly I learned by watching and listening to the ways in which they interacted with their sons. I realized that having my father involved in my life could have made my journey somewhat smoother, and I envied the other kids. I would look at them and think, *I wish I had that in my life,* but that was out of my control.

I wasn't angry or bitter anymore. It encouraged me to work hard and put myself in a position to have a close relationship with my child or children one day. Maybe I could do better.

After my parents divorced, Mom worked as a secretary and bookkeeper to take care of us. My brother and sisters had their sets of friends and did their own thing, which made me feel that I had to fend for myself, too. Given that my curious mind was fascinated with learning new things, subconsciously I sought opportunities that would help me discover what I loved and who I was meant to be.

———

One summer afternoon, I was walking into the school cafeteria for a Boy Scouts troop meeting when I noticed a guy getting into a beautiful silver Mercedes-Benz that glistened as the sun hit it. My inquisitiveness got the best of me, and I couldn't help but walk up to him and ask, "Sir, how do you get a car like that?"

He released a genuine smile, tossed the keys in his hand, and said, "Get into real estate." At the time, I was too young to understand the significance of what he meant, but it captivated me enough to retain that piece of advice. What I realized was that if I wanted quality things, I had to work for them. I didn't have an issue with working hard because I wasn't lazy. Our lawn always looked nice because I'd get up early and cut it. If I was going to have a Mercedes-Benz one day, well, I had to start somewhere. Dreams weren't going to produce reality on their own. The next time I finished cutting our yard, I looked around for prospects and found one just a couple of houses down. I wiped the sweat off my brow, smoothed out my blue and white plaid shirt, and knocked on my neighbor's front door. When she answered, I gave her my sales pitch.

"Good morning, ma'am. I just finished cutting our yard and I noticed your grass is getting tall. Would you like me to cut it?"

She looked past me at her lawn and mumbled, "Sure."

Our push mower was old, but it worked well enough to do the job right. When I finished, the lady came to the door and evaluated her yard while I watched the corners of her mouth turn upward and her eyes display approval. She grabbed her purse off the sofa, reached into her wallet, and counted ten single dollar bills into my hand. Mowing one yard inspired me to acquire two yards, and before I knew it, I had four yards. I continued going up one side of the street and down the other, asking my neighbors for their business—while mine kept growing.

In a bright yellow house just six houses down from ours, I met Mr. Van Ornum. He was an older gentleman who ran a lawn mower repair business out of his garage. I'd walk past his house and often see him sitting on a stool at an old wooden table working on a lawn mower. Whenever I waved to Mr. Van Ornum, he'd peek over his black-framed eyeglasses and nod back. When my lawn mower broke, I pushed it down the street to Mr. Van Ornum, and he fixed it. When it broke again, I bought a used one from him for thirty dollars. It didn't take long before I taught myself how to take a lawn mower apart and fix it. For my school project, I put a Briggs & Stratton lawn mower engine on a piece of wood, disassembled it in front of the class, put it back together, and started it.

I saved the majority of the money I earned and reinvested a portion of it into my business. I was actually proud of myself for taking the initiative to do it on my own. One morning, I slipped a wad of cash into the front pocket of my blue jeans and went to school. During third period, I pulled the money out and started counting it at my desk. They were mostly single dollar bills, but I wanted my classmates to see that the kid they made fun of wasn't poor anymore. I didn't make a lot of money back then, but it was a lot for my age.

The teacher smiled and kindly inquired, "Chuckie, where did you get all that money?"

Her pleasant demeanor caused me to release a warm smile when I replied, "I earned it."

"Put that away," she insisted as she walked past me, gently tapping my shoulder.

The kids were looking at me with curiosity, but no one uttered a word. It felt good to not be poor, but more importantly, I took pride in the fact that I enjoyed working. I didn't bother anyone in school because I didn't like being bothered. I had a small group of friends I'd hang out and listen to music with, but for the most part, I was a quiet kid. At that age, the only thing I wanted was for bullies and mean kids to leave me alone.

Most of the kids labeled Kevin as the strongest and toughest bully in the fifth grade. I could see why. When Kevin frowned, his eyebrows scrunched together and he looked like Butch, the bully in *The Little Rascals*. Whenever he saw me going in the same direction, he'd jump behind me, continually shoving his hand in the center of my back, discharging exaggerated undulations of laugher as I repeatedly stumbled my way down the hallway. If I turned to go in the opposite direction, he'd trip me. Kevin was worse than Frederick. When his little brain told him to hit me, he'd ball up his fist and sock me for no reason. One random weekday in class, Kevin announced that he was going to beat me up after school, and word spread like a fast-moving virus. Kids I didn't know were shouting down the corridor, "Kevin and Chuckie are going to fight after school," making a big deal out of nothing. I didn't know why we were fighting, and I didn't want to fight, but I was ready.

After school, a large assemblage of kids followed us off the school property and gathered in a circle. In seconds, Kevin and I went at it, exchanging vicious punches without either of us retreating. I felt exactly like Ralphie Parker in *A Christmas Story*, who got picked on by the bully Scut Farkus. Eventually, his emotions took over and he just beat him up. I fought with every bit of fury I had because I decided I wasn't getting beat up by Kevin or anyone else. He fought back but, in the end, I beat his ass. Several minutes later, Kevin's dad arrived to pick him up from school and found us in the center of the crowd. Kevin's father didn't say anything to either of us, but he grabbed Kevin by the back of his shirt collar, firmly walked Kevin away, and shoved him into the passenger side of his red Corvette. He appeared to be disappointed in his son's behavior. After that, Kevin never bothered me again.

I was exhausted from bullies thinking I was an easy target, and I felt I had to set a precedent to make them stop. My parents were going through a divorce, Dad had abandoned us, and my head was in another place, but I didn't take my frustrations out on anyone.

I made sure I didn't fight on school property so I wouldn't get suspended or end up back in counseling, but Clarence Bell heard about the fight. Mr. Bell was one of my fifth-grade teachers and a black belt in karate, which he taught at the YMCA. For some reason, he'd taken a liking to me, though I think we both knew I was on track to be a pretty bad kid. When I returned to school the following day, Mr. Bell pulled me aside to address the fight and then advised, "I want you to stop fighting and take karate at the YMCA. Karate will help you with structure and self-discipline." Mr. Bell didn't want me to go through life fighting. He explained, "You don't want other kids to bait you into fights. That will change you into someone you don't want to become."

I didn't like the person I was becoming, nor did I know how to prevent it, so I told Mom what Mr. Bell had recommended, and we took his advice. I signed up for karate and used money from lawn mowing to pay for it.

Mr. Bell was right; karate gave me the discipline I needed and turned me around. After participating for a few years and competing in tournaments, I never got into another fight. I had nothing to prove.

I'd been cutting grass with old mowers and steadily growing my business. When I was in sixth grade, Mom took me to Sears with her, and I ventured off to look at the lawn mowers. I laid eyes on a gold lawn mower that had a white sticker stating the finance charge was only seventeen dollars a month. Two yards would cover that, so I asked Mom if she would co-sign on the mower with me. Mom knew I was reliable. She agreed under the condition that I made every payment on time.

That gold lawn mower was faster, better, and it didn't break. With all the new business I acquired, I wore that thing out. My volume grew until I reached the point of cutting grass seven days a week, ten hours a day over the summer. During the academic year, as soon as I got home from school, I headed out to cut grass. When I had Boy Scouts, I mowed lawns in the evening and worked on projects in between. I stayed active because I enjoyed working. Properties that needed my service surrounded me, but I wasn't greedy. I didn't take on so much business that I couldn't do it all and do it properly. As much as I wanted to make money, money wasn't my motivation. Building a business on the strength of my reputation for doing excellent work inspired me. I found value in the way my customers responded to having a beautiful lawn and the income came from that.

It took me a year to pay off that gold lawn mower. Then I realized I could cut even faster if I had a riding mower. The blade width was twice as wide, so I'd cut grass in less time, and payments were only twenty-five dollars a month. I had an excellent track record with Mom, so she agreed to co-sign on that one, too. When I cut grass, I'd drive the riding mower down the street, pulling my other lawn mower in my left hand. I used the push mower to mow around trees, bushes and shrubs to make sure my lawns were as nice as possible, without a single dandelion in sight. My business expanded because my production doubled.

When I stood on the sidewalk and looked at the lawns on our street, they were uniformly manicured. Taking pride in my work, I'd smile at a job well done. At one point, I cut grass for almost every house on my street. I learned that as long as I focused on remaining productive and conscientious about my work, I would make money. The only thing that limited my ability to work was sunlight. On the days that I didn't have school, I started cutting grass at 7:00 a.m., and it never felt like work. As soon as the blades hit the grass, it caused distress and the grass released organic compounds called leaf volatiles, the scent of freshly cut grass. I loved that smell.

When I turned fourteen, I decided to put my money in the bank to keep it from slipping through my hands. Atlantic Bank was right up the street from our house; I thought they would take better care of my money. Since I was underage, the only type of account they allowed me to open was a joint one with Mom, and that was fine with me. I bought a lime green motocross bike that I rode to the bank to make deposits every week, and then I'd ride over to Burger King, get a forty-nine-cent hamburger, and go to the burger bar to pile on the fixings, making my burger gigantic and even more delicious. I had a bank account, a successful lawn mowing business, and karate had taught me discipline. Then I picked up an activity that I really enjoyed—roller skating. Life was good and I was happy.

It was during that period that I not only learned what time management was but that it was necessary. I realized I'd taken on too many activities. I had school, work, and then one activity or project after another. After four years in the Boy Scouts, I decided it was time for me to move on, confident that I'd continue accomplishing whatever goals I set. Working hard and being respected inspired me to be a better version of myself. I felt good doing honest work and not having to ask Mom to buy me things; that independence fed my passion.

———

I sat in my eighth-grade career class excited about the question my teacher, Mr. Craig, had presented. He walked up and down each row, going from one student to the next, asking what they wanted to be when they grew up. Each kid seemed excited about their response and rattled off a profession—doctor, banker, teacher, lawyer, actor, nurse, singer, chef, baseball player, artist. I couldn't wait until my teacher asked me because I was already working. I took pride in the quality of my work and the way my customers responded. If I continued working hard, with the intent of making my customers happy, I believed I could be successful with anything I did, and I knew what I wanted to be. After each kid replied, Mr. Craig nodded his head approvingly and moved on to the next student. When he got to me, I was sitting up straight, with my hands loosely clasped together on my desk.

"Chuckie, what do you want to be?"

I smiled and replied confidently, "I want to be a millionaire."

Mr. Craig paused and looked down at me disapprovingly, as if that didn't exist. Then, he scoffed, "Chuckie, you have to be realistic. Not only will you not be a millionaire, you'll probably never meet one."

Some of the kids laughed, but his response didn't discourage me. Mr. Craig didn't know what I was capable of accomplishing, but I did. And he didn't have my vision for my life. If I remained goal-oriented, focused on establishing good habits, and did quality work rather than being driven by money—money would become the byproduct of things done well.

———•—•———

I'd been roller skating for a few years at Semoran Skateway three to five nights a week for the same price as going to a movie. I wanted to start speed skating, but I couldn't afford to buy a better-quality pair of skates because they were expensive. I was making money, but not enough to spend on a hobby when my objective was to save. The wheels on the skates were Hugger wheels and cost a hundred dollars a set. The skating rink sold them, and I was sure they were marking them up. I came up with the idea to start a business and call it Chuck's Skate Shop. I thought about the way I'd operate my business, wrote down a plan, and then I began.

I got the name of the skates off the box and wrote down the type of wheels that were on the skates, along with the name of the manufacturer. I called the manufacturer, and after speaking with them as the owner of Chuck's Skate Shop, they mailed a price list to our house.

When I reviewed the wholesale prices, I couldn't wait to call in the first order for a pair of skates and wheels; they were half the retail price. I bought the wheels for forty dollars and sold them for seventy, while the skating rink continued to sell them for one hundred dollars. For the next year and a half, I turned a profit selling the wheels to kids who were regular customers at the rink, and I used some of the money to pay for my skates.

I'd removed the only obstacle that could have kept me from practicing and competing as much as I did. But when the manager found out I was responsible for his declining sales, he told me that I could no longer sell skates at Semoran Skateway. He brought an abrupt end to Chuck's Skate Shop when he called the wholesaler and explained what had transpired. The option he gave the wholesaler was that they would supply either him or me, but not both. They chose him. I learned the benefit of buying wholesale. Once you learn wholesale, you never get it out of your head. Profit is made in the difference between wholesale and retail.

My lawn mowing business was a blessing because I couldn't legally work other jobs until I turned fifteen and a half. Once I did, I added a summer job at Chuck E. Cheese to my schedule. I was the mouse, I made pizza, and I had to punch a time clock. That same summer, I briefly worked for John's Custom Air doing ductwork. My manager gave me a ride to work and drove me home because I wasn't old enough to drive. I still wasn't making a lot of money, but I enjoyed working.

I continued skating competitively and practicing at the rink seven days a week for three hours a day until I was seventeen. The time and effort I put into practicing paid off. I won several local competitions and the Southern Regional Championships in dance skating. I went on to compete in the national championships.

Although Chuck's Skate Shop had cut into the skating rink's business, one day the manager told me that he actually respected my ingenuity and work ethic. I was sixteen when he offered me the position as the DJ at the skating rink on Saturdays, and I was thrilled. I loved music, so I didn't hesitate to accept the opportunity. I was never late for work and remained conscientious about doing a great job. It wasn't long before they made me their regular DJ. I catered to the clientele, playing all the best seventies and eighties pop music, which kept them happy.

I remember when Michael Jackson came to town in 1983 and stayed at the Royal Plaza Hotel. He had just done the "Billy Jean" video and "Thriller" was about to be released. I was listening to the radio when they mentioned that Michael loved Walt Disney World, and there was a Michael Jackson Suite at the Royal Plaza Hotel in Lake Buena Vista. I called one of my friends and suggested that we go to the hotel and see if we could meet Michael Jackson. When Melanie and I walked through the front doors of the hotel, Michael was standing just fifteen feet in front of us with his mom and director John Landis. His bodyguards were nearby, but as soon as one of them turned away, we walked over to him, and I said, "Michael, I'm a disc jockey at the skating rink in town, and I play your music all the time. I just wanted to meet you."

His bodyguards flanked us in an attempt to prevent me from talking to him any further. Michael intervened, kindly motioning with his hand to both men as he gently assured them, "No, they're fine." Masses of people were entering the hotel lobby, and Michael suggested, "Why don't you two come upstairs with us."

Our eyes widened and our cheeks rose as we followed them into the elevator and up to a private suite with his name and signature on the door. The suite was massive. Melanie and I sat on the sofa while Michael showed us his pictures and told us about his upcoming tour. An hour and a half later, he gave me his phone number and said that if I needed anything, to call. I didn't want anything from him, so I never called, but he was really nice to us. Michael's "Thriller" video came out a few days later, and the kids at the rink couldn't get enough of it. I went to see his Victory Tour at the Gator Bowl in Jacksonville, and it blew me away.

While I was a few years removed from the bullying and teasing, it had an impact, and I kept working to be the best version of myself. Turning sixteen opened the door to having more freedom because Mom and Ron, her new husband, gave me a red, faded 1967 Volkswagen Bug with a hole in the floor. It didn't have a radio or air conditioning, but it worked and it was mine. I bought my clothing, so I could dress better. A preppy friend of mine and I started buying Izod shirts, and I bought a pair of white Reebok high-tops. After wearing those shirts a few times, and gaining popularity as a DJ, I was considered one of the preppy kids in school.

In between being a DJ and my lawn care business, I worked evenings at John's Exxon gas station. Since so many people were working for someone else, I thought that I would make more having a paycheck than running my own business. But I found that wasn't the case.

At seventeen, I stopped working at the gas station and concluded it was time to move on from my lawn mowing business. Skating had gone well for me, and I had reached the point where I had to test my skills and skate competitively as a professional skater or pursue a path in business. Business fascinated me, and I had to see where that path would lead, so I decided to stop skating.

I did a good job at the skating rink and constantly interacted with people; that led to building traction as a DJ. Before I was old enough to drink, I was hired as the DJ at some of the best nightclubs in town. I worked consistently, but I wasn't able to save much. To be in demand as a DJ, it was a requirement to have the type of music people wanted to hear, and as a result, I was always in town at the record shop continually buying new music. In addition to buying my clothes, I reinvested my income into DJ equipment and purchased a car that I made payments on. Paying for food, gas, and other incidentals kept me from saving much, but I loved what I was doing. Working for others taught me that I didn't want to work for anyone other than myself.

It's not over until you stop. Move on, knowing there is something better in front of you.

—CHUCK WHITTALL

Chapter 2

Defining Who You Are

I didn't have a clear path regarding what I wanted to be after high school, but as I came closer to graduating, I heard kids intermittently discussing the advice they were given relating to preparation for college, career advice, networking, their image, and other things. Over time, guidance and expertise appeared to have a positive effect. Many of my classmates graduated from Winter Park High School and went to college to pursue their ambitions and specific areas of study, while I tried to learn more on my own.

I would have appreciated having a mentor to discuss career options with, or who would take me inside of their business to show me how it worked. Perhaps I would have begun to flourish sooner and avoided making poor choices. Having a mentor wouldn't necessarily have meant I'd take every piece of advice I was given, but it might have created more options.

I've observed mentors who inspired others with their knowledge, passion, and expertise—wrapped with purposeful intent.

That's the way it ought to be. We should want to pass along what we know, provide opportunities for those seeking them, and lift others to see over walls to view the vast opportunities they may not have otherwise been aware existed.

When people asked me who my mentor was, I felt uncomfortable replying, "Other than my drive to succeed, I didn't have one." My mentor wasn't an individual; it was always hard work and drive that propelled me to the next level. Of course, I've received great advice, but I didn't have a trusted advisor or anyone continually guiding or helping me. With the problems that adolescents are facing today, they need supportive guidance to help them be confident and optimistic about life, learn how to work through challenges, formulate better relationships with their peers, make healthy lifestyle choices, and establish goals.

As my vision became more defined, I advanced by surrounding myself with great people—wise people I could learn from. I had an innate drive to do well, and I wasn't willing to back down or give up on anything. The network that you create or become a part of contributes to or detracts from your level of success. I developed a hunger for success that wouldn't subside. Perhaps some of my prosperity was due to the fact that I didn't have anyone to work with me.

College wasn't a part of my plan, and when I made that choice, I never felt inferior because I didn't pursue a degree. I felt college would teach me how to work for someone, and I didn't want that, so I created my own path. I sought inspiration and devoured it. That helped me define who I was and who I was working to become. I had an entrepreneurial spirit, work ethic, and the ability to put myself in a position so people wouldn't make fun of me for being disadvantaged. When I asked myself how I could change my situation, the answer was simple: work. It was *always* work. I didn't make a choice not to go to college to circumvent learning; I loved learning. I didn't decide to become an entrepreneur so I could have the freedom *not* to work. Working for myself meant that I would work more because I had yet to satisfy my appetite. I had a multitude of riveting ideas to sift through in the process, and I needed to see them through. I didn't take several different jobs because I was trying to make money any way I could. I took them because I was trying to determine *who I was*. The answer: *an entrepreneur.*

If I started another business, I wanted to do something I was good at and loved doing. I possessed a keen perception when it came to what teenagers wanted from working at the skating rink and being one. I was good at being a DJ, loved music, passionate about starting another business, and I paid attention to where I saw a demand. I thought teenagers wanted more options than going to the movies and skating. Even though kids couldn't legally drink, they still wanted an alternative.

My buddy Mark Salmon and I decided to open a young-adult club called Odyssey. We found a location, met with the landlord, shared our vision with him, and he agreed that we had a good idea. The landlord took a chance and rented the space to us. We had half the money required to secure the building and set up the club, but we needed an investor for the other half. I went to my network and asked around. A lady who owned the day care that my brother attended when he was younger gave us the investment in exchange for 50 percent of the business. The three of us agreed that Mark and I would co-manage the club, and I would be the DJ.

Mark and I did a lot of work to get the club ready, and we hired people to help us. When we opened, we charged a five-dollar entry fee and had a concession stand serving soft drinks and hot dogs. The first night we were open, everyone paid cash, and we exceeded our expectations. We operated five nights a week from 7:00 p.m. until 1:00 a.m. and started each night with a line of anxious teens cramming the sidewalks, waiting to get in. Odyssey became the teen hot spot in town, and that line stretched down the street. At the end of the night, Mark and I fed leftover hot dogs to the alligator in the lake behind the building rather than waste them.

A few months after opening, our growing business was interrupted when the ceiling of Odyssey caved in. Prior to Mark and I taking occupancy, there had been a fire in the building and the ceiling hadn't been properly restored. Unfortunately, the landlord never disclosed this to us. No one was hurt, but our other partner was upset because the three of us were responsible for repairs if we wanted to continue operating. Mark and I accepted that it was out of our control, but our partner refused to pay for any damage and sued us. Mark and I defended ourselves in court and won because the judge said the plaintiff's case was without merit. Faced with the decision to move forward or give up, Mark and I cleaned up the place, repaired the ceiling, and tried to recover the business, but in the end, it was lost. From this error in judgment, I learned to personally do a thorough walk-through before investing in any property.

———

Being that I didn't want to remain where I was for the rest of my life, I couldn't accept having a complacent mindset; it would only threaten my progress. My father's absence encouraged me to figure things out and determine where I wanted to land. Indirectly, that helped me become stronger and more focused on being the kind of person I wanted to be.

Over the years, I've learned firsthand that we all have something to offer, and it is left to each of us to elect what that contribution will be. For me, the point of working hard is not to accumulate wealth; it's about pursuing dreams, achieving goals, personal development, positioning myself to take great care of my family, and helping others. It's about maximizing my time here and leaving nothing undone. When you are blessed, bless others by paying it forward.

It can take some time before we master certain things, and there will be countless others we never will. When we are able to pass those lessons along and reveal our own errors, it can be beneficial to others:

1. Lead by example.
2. Don't be afraid to confront poor behavior.
3. Show interest and study people so you can effectively offer them good ideas.
4. Refrain from being combative in your communication and offer advice without being critical.
5. Take the time to *listen* to what people have to say.
6. Positively impact lives and elevate people to the next level.

My mother had been divorced for a few years, and when I was fifteen, she married Ron, a family and marriage counselor. On account of that, we moved a couple of miles away from the home we'd grown up in. Regardless of how hard I worked, Ron lectured me about something nearly every day. Being an entrepreneur wasn't a real job to him, and he didn't have any respect for me for not wanting to attend college. His recommendation was that

I should get a real job. The day after I turned eighteen, without forewarning, my stepfather announced, "Son, you're eighteen— you need to move out."

"When?" I asked.

"Today," he replied as if I should have known. But I didn't. I hadn't been planning to live at home much longer, but there had never been any discussion about moving out when I turned eighteen. If there had been, I would have prepared for it.

"Really?" I asked flatly, processing his time frame. Ron didn't reply.

I don't think he ever cared for me much, but I came with the package. Over the years, Mom had displayed a great deal of respect for the way I worked and kept to my commitments. She trusted me. When I turned seventeen, my mother co-signed so that I could purchase a beautiful white 1971 240Z. I learned about the power of credit at a young age, and I was never late on a single payment. I wasn't going to let Mom down or have Ron say, "I told you so." When Ron found out, he was furious with Mom, and I don't think he ever let it go. Asking me to leave was a part of his lingering anger.

That day, my mother's expression appeared as if she had been denied the only thing she ever asked of Ron, but she couldn't change her husband's decision, and, respectfully, I didn't expect her to. After Ron announced his decision, Mom quietly turned away and walked toward the hallway, taking slow steps. There was nothing else for me to say, so I shifted my mind into survival mode and obediently went to gather my belongings. I was resolute that I'd figure things out and quickly find a place to live. Visibly upset, Mom opened the door to the linen closet and reached inside. "Take these," she insisted with a wistful glance, placing a top and bottom sheet in my hands. I calmly walked into the bathroom, grabbed my toothbrush and toothpaste, and then went across the hall into my bedroom. I scanned my room one last time, grabbed a stack of folded clothes from the dresser drawer, and left. Although Tammy was no longer living at home, I didn't get a chance to say goodbye to Tim and Heather.

I drove a couple of miles up the street, trying to decide where to begin. When I saw a red and white For Rent sign on the lawn of an apartment complex, I pulled into the parking lot. At the very least, I needed to know what it would take to rent an apartment and then find somewhere to sleep that night. I went inside the office and introduced myself to the girl behind the desk. I told her I'd seen their sign and asked about the apartment they had available. She told me they were running a one hundred-dollar move-in special, which is all I had on me. Then she showed me a studio apartment. It wasn't anything special, but it had the basics. Since I had to work that night, I didn't have much time to look around. I filled out the application, paid the hundred-dollar fee, and asked if I could move in immediately. Half an hour later, she gave me the keys, and I settled in with the few items I had in my car.

I stopped by the local movie theater to give one of my buddies my new address. He ran into the back room and came out handing me a large box of toilet paper. I left the theater and went to the grocery store, bought a fresh loaf of Merita bread, a pack of Oscar Mayer Thick Cut Bologna, and a jar of Miracle Whip. I went home and sat on the floor of my empty apartment, eating a bologna sandwich. I had to save money to pay bills and furnish the place, so delicious bologna sandwiches would have to be enough for a while. I was prepared to make do.

When I finished working at the club that night, I drove over to our old house. I didn't stop; I slowly passed while reminiscing about the little home I had grown up in. I recalled playful moments wrestling with Mom, weeding the yard with her over lighthearted conversations, and comfortably sitting together on the sofa watching television. I could see myself rushing through the door to the aroma of Mom's tacos wafting up my nostrils, or sitting down to a plate of hot dogs and potato chips with my family.

I was grateful for that house and the memories created there. This time, the house was different. Everything was pitch black, as though that part of my life had ended. It was time to build the life I wanted—the way I envisioned it. I gradually accelerated and continued down the street, with a heaviness swelling in my chest.

I opened the door to my apartment, flipped on the light switch, and closed the door behind me. My eyes wandered around the empty space as I slipped out of my gym shoes. I removed the sheets from the kitchen counter, traded them for my car keys, and spread them out on the floor. When I shut off the lights, I laid down, resting my hands behind my head as a pillow, only to stare at the ceiling in a silent room that had a magnetic pull on my thoughts. I was intent on changing my lifestyle, but for now, I had to start somewhere. As hard as it was getting thrown out of the house, it turned out to be the best thing for me. I'd manage my money better and continue working toward who I wanted to be. Before long I drifted off, thinking, *I'm going through the process of trial and error, but it's not going to be this way forever.*

———•———

Being in pursuit of your destiny or trying to ascertain how you will shape your life doesn't mean it should be unpleasant or stressful. That's why it's essential to maintain balance during the process. Music was therapeutic and it did that for me. As a result, I continued working as a DJ, but shortly after I turned nineteen, a couple of friends presented me with an opportunity to become an investor and partner in their stucco and drywall business. I agreed and invested a portion of the income that I made as a DJ into the stucco and drywall business and added this to my list of endeavors. The problem was that there are only twenty-four hours in a day.

Waking up early was innate. Since the age of fourteen, I'd delivered monthly newspapers for a neighborhood in the Pines. Around the time that I became a disc jockey at some of the more prominent nightclubs in town, the newspaper increased my distribution area. The problem was that I worked the nightclubs until two o'clock in the morning. With a larger area, eight hundred papers needed to be delivered by 4:00 a.m. Despite the fact that I managed to get all of the papers delivered on my first day with the new route, I was thirty minutes late. I struggled to get by on an hour and a half of sleep. The following day I was late again, and my boss cautioned, "You can't be late anymore." After working twenty-two and a half hours for two days in a row, I accepted that I couldn't keep up with that pace. I wasn't managing my time appropriately and, if I continued overextending myself, I'd damage my reputation and lose my job anyway. I didn't want that as part of my job history, so I thanked my boss for the opportunity and resigned from the paper route. My lawn mowing business taught me that time management was a critical aspect of success. When the demand on my time became challenging as a DJ, I hired other DJs to work for me and then placed them at the clubs that wanted me for a percentage of their pay. I enjoyed all of my other jobs for different reasons, but spinning records and interacting with the crowd was the most fun.

Working as a DJ played an instrumental part in helping to cultivate my networking and public speaking skills, which have proven to be indispensable in business. You are a brand and you must be able to promote your own brand. When I'm speaking, it's important for people to feel that I am confident and that they have my personal attention. I learned how to speak to a room of five hundred people as though I am speaking to a single person. I also found that asking the right questions and learning more about the business side of what you are doing can help create other opportunities. Often people focus on doing their job instead of understanding the full scope of the business; however, that's where professional growth comes into play.

———•••———

Initially, my partners and I were making money here and there in the stucco and drywall business, but it had its drawbacks when it came to being paid on time, or even getting paid at all. I suppose it was the nature of the beast, and we kept working, anticipating that it would change. Fortunately, having a dual income allowed me to sustain my lifestyle and continue pushing through with the stucco and drywall.

Time and a lack of experience gave rise to one harsh lesson after another. The stucco and drywall business struggled, and we went $100,000 in debt. I spoke with my partners and proposed that they could walk away and I'd take over the business, assuming all the debt. They accepted the offer. I had enough infrastructure that I thought I could turn it around. I anticipated the first few years on my own would be challenging, but I forged ahead, given that I was learning the business from the ground up. After I took over, I made money, lost a few more deals, and struggled some more, but I needed to be resilient and somehow find a way to persevere.

I was doing better financially, but I was working from one end of the day into the next. After a little over a year of being on my own, I moved into a nice villa and bought a 1978 silver convertible Mercedes-Benz with a red interior. I never forgot the guy with the Mercedes. I got the car, but it was his advice that was still looming. *"Get into real estate."*

———•———

A year and a half later, I was standing in line at the bank making a deposit for my stucco and drywall business when I met Ronna, a super-hot girl with beautiful, long brown hair and a stunning smile. We started dating when I was twenty, and our relationship organically evolved into something quite special. A year later, Ronna and I were married. We worked together with the stucco and drywall business, but we hadn't made much money. My DJ income was what kept me afloat in in the interim, but after we got married, I gave it up because I didn't think being a DJ would work well for our marriage.

When we moved into our apartment, we had some furniture, but we didn't have a dining room table. We went to Burdines department store and saw a table for $99 but couldn't afford it. Every Saturday, Ronna and I went to Burdines, and we'd look at that table. Ronna would sigh and say, "I really like that table," but we could barely pay our power bill. Four months later, we bought that $99 table. Although it's in storage, we still have it today. It's one of those things that reminds me of where I came from. Things were difficult back then, and I haven't forgotten that $99 was important to us then, and it is now.

My wife and I started buying and selling foreclosed homes from the government. We fixed them up—painted, landscaped, and then sold them. Ronna and I were getting by, making do with what little we had. Ronna's mother, Reba, often invited us to dinner because she knew we were struggling and that was her way of helping us. If we weren't eating at Reba's house, our standard meal was macaroni and cheese, hot dogs or both for nearly a year. Neither of us complained because we believed that if we kept working, things would get better one day. A year later, the landlord raised our rent. Ronna and I decided we couldn't afford the rent, and it was more advantageous to invest in buying a two-bedroom house in Winter Springs.

I usually went by the house to see Mom, and one afternoon we were sitting at the kitchen table catching up. She asked how business was going, and I told her about some of the situations that occurred and what we were dealing with. As I explained why we were still struggling with our stucco and drywall company, Ron walked in the kitchen rubbing his fingers through his long white Santa Claus beard.

"You need to quit being in business," he began. "Go get a job at McDonald's and work your way up. Then get a mail truck and drive that around instead of that fancy car."

I didn't say anything to him. Instead, I thought, *I'll never do that*. I'm going to stay in business. How would I accomplish anything if I quit every time I faced adversity? I might not be successful all the time, but I'm not going to quit and give up. That wasn't the first time it happened, and it might not be the last, but somehow I'd work through it. I wasn't convinced that the stucco and drywall business would be a lasting career, but I was gaining knowledge from that line of work, and it was challenging me to find solutions. I did the opposite of what Ron advised and continued with C.W. Diversified, my stucco and drywall business.

I was optimistic about the stucco and drywall business because I had great communication skills and I knew I could sell our services. And while I owned the business, I didn't do the work; I piecemealed the jobs out. Typically, the crew was paid

$1,500 or so for doing a job. In addition, we were taking on and completing both residential and commercial business.

After we were able to save enough money, we invested everything we had into a bigger job. The company we completed the project for went out of business. We didn't get paid, and we didn't have the resources to pay our workers. Our reputation was everything, and the fact that others could walk away from their responsibilities was devastating.

—◦—

We took all the money we made on residential projects and, once again, bought into a big job for $72,000. We completed the entire job within the thirty-day billing cycle, and it took every single dollar we had; it was critical to get our investment back. One week after another, the company put us off, saying they were taking care of it, and then that company filed bankruptcy, leaving us with nothing. My little brother, Timothy, loaned me $100 to pay our power bill. I recall the day my wife and I pulled up to a Circle K convenience store and gas station. Before I got out of the car to pump the gas, she turned to me and asked, "What do you want me to do? Should I sell my wedding ring?"

I looked in Ronna's gentle, beautiful eyes as she slowly twisted her gold ring, ready to take it off and hand it to me to sell. Ronna handled the books and knew where we were financially, but that told me my wife believed we would get through this, too. In the midst of the uncertainty and hardship we were facing, Ronna's faith in me was unfaltering.

"You're *not* selling your ring."

Although it was particularly stressful because we didn't have any money, I believed there was a solution, and I was determined to find it. We had applied for an American Express credit card and, by the grace of God, it came in the mail that same day. We used that card to fill up the gas tank, knowing we had a month to pay it off. I drove my wife home and told her, "I'm not coming home until I figure this out."

I drove from builder to builder and one house to another asking for their business. Then I called one of the builders that we conducted business with and asked, "Steve, do you have any houses that need stucco? Anything?"

He said, "Yeah, I've got one in Tuscawilla."

He gave me the address, and I went over to the house and took measurements. Then I called him and said, "I measured your house and it's a $5,500 job. But I really need some money right now. If you'll give me $3,500 in advance, I'll complete the job for you at cost. But, Steve, I need the check today."

His response was, "Come by my house and pick it up."

Steve agreed because of my track record. He trusted me. I went home and told my wife, "Honey, we can pay our mortgage payment and we can buy groceries. We'll use the rest of the money to finance the job." Completing that job helped us get rolling again, and we didn't have to sell my wife's wedding ring.

Three years later, we had over 110 employees at the stucco and drywall company. We did a lot of small jobs and we did them well. We did what we said we would do and worked to exceed expectations. We were consistent, likable, and acted with integrity. When our reputation had grown, we were offered an impressive opportunity—the convention center at the World Center Marriott. Part of being successful is knowing when to move on to the next level of whatever you're doing. If you're not moving forward, you're not progressing. Taking each valuable lesson with me, I left the stucco and drywall business. I had more to offer, and the vision I had was building homes.

While doing stucco and drywall, several of the home builders didn't have the money to pay us. I wasn't willing to continue on that path. The solution to alleviate the problem of not getting paid would be to build homes myself. This way, I could ensure the people who worked for me were properly taken care of in the process. I went to a trade school and earned my general contractor's license. At that time, Ronna and I still had income from flipping houses and thought it was time to build ourselves a house. We learned a great deal and were confident that we knew how to do it right, so we began. Our house was coming along beautifully and, halfway through the process, a guy came to me and said, "I'd like to buy that house from you." I'd barely convinced the bank to give me a loan for $135,000, though we sold the house for $195,000 before it was even finished. The great thing was that not only did we sell that house, I had five other people who asked us to build them a house, and so we did. I paid attention to every minute detail we put into each home, making sure that when we were done, each of them was a home that Ronna and I would have loved to live in. Taking care in building one beautiful and quality home created five additional opportunities.

After building homes for a couple of years, I met someone who wanted to be partners, and I thought we could grow the business together. This lasted for about a year. One day I called and asked where he was. He casually admitted that he was home reading the paper and drinking coffee; meanwhile, I was out in the heat pouring concrete. I told him I was the one who was always working—we couldn't be partners anymore. This was my third partnership, and the only partner who'd worked as hard as I was my buddy Mark, who had opened the teen night club with me. I realized that the others didn't have the same work ethic as I did. Unless you are equally yoked, someone is always doing more work. The person who works the hardest may be resentful, and I was running harder on the hamster wheel. When one partner isn't putting in the effort, the other may begin to think he or she shouldn't either. Then your business suffers. When you're an entrepreneur, you're on your own. You get paid for what you do.

Among the first few homes I built was one I completed for a young businessman, Michael Tannous. He and his father, Suhail Tannous, were very happy with his home. Suhail Tannous was a really nice man who appreciated the quality of my work and the way I conducted business. He said, "I would like to invest with you in building more houses, and I want you to build a house for me."

"Mr. Tannous, I appreciate that, but I don't have much money. These homes are presales," I confessed.

"I'll loan you the cash to build spec homes. Whatever you sell them for—we'll just split it fifty-fifty," he proposed.

We agreed on a handshake.

Every Friday, I would go to Mr. Tannous's house, tell him how much I needed, and he would give it to me. It didn't take long before we had a few houses being built. In a couple of years, we had built several custom homes. My company, Pristine Custom Homes, became one of the largest custom-home builders in Central Florida. Due to the success we were having, I outstripped Mr. Tannous's resources. Everything we did was on a handshake. When he was paid his profits, he never questioned me. *When people trust you, work not to lose it.*

All of my businesses to that point were really just work and education. When I got into the homebuilding business, it was my first venture into creativity. Consequently, I started creating beautiful homes and sold them like crazy. Pristine Homes was a glamorous business where I built custom homes for wealthy people. Every time I built a home, it was a mini masterpiece.

Pristine Homes was a true business. I hired several vendors, set up accounts, and dealt with financial institutions. The process taught me the importance of net worth, how to leverage capital, and how to deliver a quality product. When people are buying a second or third home, they are more likely to point out every imperfection. So when I built homes, I did my own walk-throughs so that I could ensure nothing was wrong. I carried that practice with me.

I learned construction in the homebuilding business, and in fact, I had to learn every aspect of the business. Although I am ultimately responsible, I hired experts. When you're in charge, the buck stops with you. When you accept the gratification for doing something right, accept the blame for doing something wrong. People will judge you by the examples you set. A characteristic of being humble is giving credit to your people rather than blaming them. It is a single-edged sword.

Over the next few years, Pristine Homes achieved the status of building million-dollar homes, which was a lot of money back then. Given that we were doing well, my wife and I decided we would build ourselves a million-dollar home without incurring debt. At the time we started construction on our home, we had approximately ten other homes going. When our house was 90 percent finished, I realized the money for the project was nearly depleted.

I remember the night I went into the kitchen and told my wife, "You know that new home we're building in Heathrow?"

"Yes," she replied calmly.

"We can't afford it. I just figured out how much money we need to finish it and what we owe on the other projects. Ronna, we've got to sell it."

She paused and looked at me for a moment then replied softly, "If that's what we've got to do, that's what we've got to do."

When you have that kind of support from your spouse, it makes difficult decisions more palatable. Ronna and I put our house up for sale and moved into a $400,000 spec home we'd built. It was our practice to ensure our homes were quality and something we would want to live in, and as it was absolutely beautiful, we did. We sold our house to this guy from Minnesota and went under contract for $995,000. Considering we were running out of money and I wasn't going to close on his house for sixty to ninety days, I took a short-term note out on the house with Sun-Trust and borrowed $300,000 against the nearly million-dollar home so I could put more capital into my company. What I didn't foresee was that the guy from Minnesota was a shyster.

He called me and blatantly proclaimed, "Chuck, I'm not going to close on the house."

"What do you mean you're not going to close?" I thought he was joking.

"I've changed my mind. I'm not closing."

"If you're serious, that's fine, then I'll sell it to someone else."

"But I'm not going away that easily," he added with a slight pause as if he were contemplating his next statement. "I want a five hundred-thousand-dollar discount on the house," he demanded.

"The house practically cost what I'm selling it to you for. I'm not discounting it!"

Again, he brazenly insisted on a half-million-dollar discount as though I didn't have a choice other than to oblige him, and still I refused. In a move I hadn't calculated, the guy went to the bank and bought my mortgage note on the house. Now, I owed $300,000. I couldn't believe *this* was happening, and the guy wasn't done; he then tried to foreclose in the most egregious act. I realized that, from the onset, this guy from Minnesota had devised a strategy to steal this million-dollar house from me for $300,000. I was thrust into a terrible predicament because all of my money was tied up in this house, and had been allocated to generate the revenue needed to continue building homes.

I didn't know what else to do other than call a family friend, Jay Stanton, who was also an attorney. And when he answered, I explained the situation without excluding a single fact. Sounding sympathetic, Jay replied, "You know what, I'm not going to let this happen. I'll even waive the legal fees."

I didn't know what the outcome would be, but at the very least, I owed Jay a debt of gratitude for taking this guy on.

Without hesitation, we filed a counterclaim to the foreclosure suit, and then waited, during which time this guy's actions were still threatening everything. A year passed from the time he bought the mortgage to the time we went to court. Being that I had been persistent in my efforts to get to that point in my career, I was paralyzed emotionally and financially. The completeness of the ordeal prompted bouts of depression that were ineludible. It was difficult to envision walking away, because it wasn't in me, but it had become arduous to sustain the stress of it all. The only thing I could do was fight through it and learn from this setback—so it would never happen again.

When we finally went to court, the judge dismissed the foreclosure, yet we still had the lawsuit. Right before we went to trial, the judge warned, "One of you is going to be very unhappy with the outcome. I am going to give you a chance to go out into the hallway and settle it."

We looked at one another and went out into the hallway. The guy's attorney asked, "Do you want to settle?"

I was exhausted, yet I'd been through so much already, I was willing to hear the judge's ruling if the guy didn't agree to return what was mine.

"I just want my house back," I replied staunchly. "You can have the three hundred thousand dollars that you put up for the mortgage, but you have to give me time to sell it. After that, we'll go our separate ways."

The guy bought the mortgage. And even though the judge dismissed the foreclosure, he was due $300,000, which the guy agreed to. I left the courtroom thankful that it was finally over, but I drove home feeling deflated. When I put the house on the market, it sold the following day for $1,050,000. I had just cashed my first million-dollar check—and it was depressing. I should have been excited and felt somewhat relieved, but the financial stress and frustration over the entire con hit me hard. I had been pulled into a fight I didn't want, just like when I was a kid. I wanted to build things that would make people happy, earn an honest living, and take pride in my work. I was twenty-seven years old, and a complete stranger had tried to take what I was building, along with my passion and purpose. That was a hard lesson to swallow.

During that fight—the protracted litigation—I went up to my room and laid across my bed. The heaviness in my chest expanded throughout my body, like concrete being poured into a hole. I didn't want to get up, go to work, or do anything. Fighting depleted my energy. I couldn't understand why this unthinkable situation or anything else had happened. Why would someone formulate a plan to shamelessly steal something from me? I didn't know that guy, nor had I done anything to him. I'd taken one devastating financial hit after another. I never considered filing bankruptcy or walking away from my responsibilities without finding a way to reconcile them. I worked hard, believing I was doing everything right. I didn't hurt or deceive anyone, yet I couldn't seem to circumvent negative situations. I refused to become what I didn't like as a means of survival, but I couldn't abandon what I believed I was meant to do. This industry—real estate—being an entrepreneur, independent, and creative in nature felt right, like it was my destiny. I was hurting because I had this intense determination burning inside of me that wouldn't subside. I was tasked with overcoming a depressed state if I were to continue, though it wasn't immediate.

It took a few months before I was ready to leave the house and get back to work. When I did, I got in my car and drove to a 7-Eleven near my home. I didn't need anything other than to force myself up and out of the house. This time was harder than the others, but I had Ronna, a beautiful home, my ability to continue working, and people who depended on me for their income. I opened my CD case, took out *Personal Power* by Anthony Robbins, inserted it into my CD player, and listened. I was inspired after listening to the first CD, and I finished the course within two weeks. And for some reason, a piece of advice that Anthony Robbins gave was to make a crazy wish list, even if it was to buy an airplane—and I did that.

I got my real estate sales license and, 366 days later, I acquired my broker's license. After that situation unfolded, I was ready to change careers. Emotions that coincide with the homebuilding business were too much. As long as my passion was still intact, I had a lot more to offer. Settling for anything less would only limit my success.

Integrity and reputation define who you are, and everyone has a choice on how they want to be perceived. I wasn't always like this; it took some time for me to establish who I wanted people to see me as. It came from studying particular characteristics or qualities that attract certain people as opposed to the characteristics that seduce others. People don't think about it, but it's important to determine what it means to be a good person and work to become that person. Have you ever taken the time to sit down and think about who you want to become versus who you are? If not, do so. If you have, ask yourself—are you the person you aspired to be?

Through it all, I kept my professional demeanor and allowed my attorney to handle the case, which he did pro bono, based on my reputation. It wasn't what I would call a win-win, but I didn't lose.

Defining yourself is an essential piece to accomplishing goals. When you walk in and out of a room, how do you want people to define you? Do you smile when you shake someone's hand? Are you a good listener? Do you care about others? Do you need to win at all costs, or are you willing to compromise for the greater good? Some people have a bad day and they're disrespectful or unpleasant in their communications, and that's what people tend to remember.

Regardless of what transpires, be the type of person you would want to do business with. I wish someone had told me that early in life. I was in my mid-thirties before I determined the distinct qualities by which I wanted people to define me. But when I established those qualities, I refused to relinquish them. When I travel and go places, even to restaurants, people don't know what

I make or what I do—but they will remember how I treat them. Being nice is how you set yourself apart.

———•———

Exiting the homebuilding business, I acquired my pilot's license in the early nineties. And because I enjoyed flying, I considered being a pilot at one point. Pilots started off around $35,000, and I was previously making a few hundred thousand a year. I loved selling, and I thought I could sell jets, as I believed selling was an instinctive trait not necessarily governed by the product you sell. However, you have to believe in what you sell.

Through research, I identified one of the best jet aircraft manufacturers at the time, Gulfstream Aerospace. In 1996, I got on the phone and bugged the hell out of the CEO of Gulfstream to give me a job interview. I called him persistently until he finally agreed. I was a member of a flying club, so I flew a Piper Cherokee to Savannah, Georgia, to interview with the senior vice president, Raynor Reavis.

"How many corporate boardrooms have you been in?" Mr. Reavis asked.

"None. But I can sell. And I can definitely sell your airplane."

That statement grabbed his attention, and we engaged in a lengthy conversation. Toward the end, Mr. Reavis said, "You know, I only have two salesmen in the United States. One for the East Coast and one for the West Coast. But we're starting a new division of shared ownerships where we sell fractions of airplanes. I'll hire you for that, if you want a job. You can move to Texas and start selling jets out there."

"Mr. Reavis, I don't want to sell pieces of jets. I want to sell whole jets."

He leaned back in his black leather chair with a decisive smile and added convincingly, "Chuck, you're really not the right person to sell jets, you're the right person to buy a jet. And one day you will. I think you should be an entrepreneur."

There are small, subtle pushes in life, and sometimes they happen for a reason. Had I interviewed with an aircraft manufacturer that wasn't as prominent as Gulfstream, they might have hired me, and I could be in an entirely different career. Mr. Reavis had met numerous private aircraft owners. He knew the type of people who purchased them and what it took to own an airplane. He was an expert in his field. I left without the offer I wanted, but I had something more valuable: his advice.

When I reached a cruising altitude, I wasn't thinking of anything. It was a beautiful day, with a mixture of clouds and blue skies. Looking down at the earth—everything was too small to worry about. Flying was an escape that disconnected me from everything below and made me appreciate the magnificent view in front of me. When I landed, I told my wife, "I need to get back into real estate and just do real estate—but I want to do a different aspect of it."

Failing is when you are unsuccessful in achieving your goal and make the decision that you are not going to accomplish something; you give up. Failing is about learning lessons, like getting the results of a test. You see what you did or didn't do correctly, and eventually you can learn to master it. Failing has a negative connotation because it sounds like finality. Reframe the way you think; learn from the failure, change what you are doing, and try again.

—CHUCK WHITTALL

Chapter 3

Determined Not to Fail

I didn't have a life preserver to hold on to, so I had no choice other than to keep my head above water and learn how to survive. Generally in life, there aren't people who say, "Let me help you out," or "Let me take care of you." I had to try different things and find my niche. Taking into account I'd made the decision not to go to college, I needed a plan, and I still needed an education because I was determined not to fail. I opted for trade schools and went to several. Trade schools are where I learned how to do the many aspects of what I'm doing now. In addition, they taught me to understand precisely what my contractors did. Knowledge is power, and the knowledge I gained from trade schools is invaluable.

Whenever someone asked where I went to college, I explained that my education came from trade schools. The response was primarily the same from one person to another and carried little to no weight—basically, trade schools were looked down upon. Trade schools provide hands-on experience that can lead to successful career alternatives; nevertheless, there's an unmerited negative stigma associated with trade schools, and it is unwarranted. College grows your knowledge of life and is directed toward several different goals; however, it doesn't go into depth for so many other careers where a college degree isn't required, such as a plumber, carpenter, or electrician. I know one of the largest electrical contractors who is extremely wealthy, and he started as an electrician. He worked his way up to owning his own company. Today, he has a private jet, a helicopter, a home in the city, and a home on the beach. Not bad for someone who went to trade school. Whether you have a degree or trade-school education, your level of drive in any industry depends on how far you are willing to go. Your limits are those you establish.

Whatever it is you want to do and however you decide to do it, there is no free ride. You've got to go out there and work your ass off. If you choose to go the distance in commercial or residential real estate, learn as much as you can, grow your business, and surround yourself with talented people. Being an entrepreneur and working in real estate development isn't for the weak; it can devour you. Focus. Be willing to move boundaries and exceed expectations. Believe me when I say, *nothing was easy.* I had to learn how to do things properly in my business. And my failures? Well, I call them learning opportunities. As far as my process, I hired contractors because I didn't physically build. Since I didn't, it was necessary to acquire my contractor's license and understand that business. It's my responsibility to know that things are being done right. You should want to know the process or what the people who work in your business know *and more.* If you don't, you can absolutely lose your shirt!

I obtained my real estate license, brokerage license, pool license, and most importantly, my Class A general contractor's license, which necessitated taking accounting classes. It was necessary to understand the legal, banking, and construction aspects as well as several other businesses to be successful in real estate. Why? Several different businesses are intertwined within it. Surprisingly, I've used nearly everything I've learned. The industry I was going into demanded that I be well versed, so I did what was necessary to be prepared. I continued growing my knowledge in the process, *and I still am*. My business is constantly evolving.

When you have your own business, you assume responsibility for it, and you have to accept that life is generally like that. I've found that a crucial component is being able to survive on your own. I did for a long time. Having to do that caused me to be more helpful and generous to other people along the way. I am able to relate to and empathize with their struggles and barriers, and I can equally identify with their passion and drive when I see it. I aim to teach people what I know, instill confidence, and encourage them to accomplish whatever it is they want to achieve. Truth be told, it doesn't take much to inspire others; people just need to know it's possible to attain their goals, and if they can see that *you've* done it, it helps.

———

Each of my businesses taught me a great deal, and I had experience in knowing *when* it was time to move on. I had gained a wealth of knowledge in various areas through career exploration, and I loved being an entrepreneur, but I wanted to be certain we were making the right decision. That particular week, when Sunday rolled around, we were in church enjoying the peaceful selection from the choir followed by our pastor, who delivered a sermon with perfect timing, as if it were divinely prepared for me: *When God Closes One Door*. I sat in the pew and took it in, smiling at Ronna as she gave my hand a light squeeze when he began.

Our pastor said, "We have to accept when a door closes. Be prepared for the next one that opens."

I was at that door.

After the service, Ronna and I went to lunch. I was no longer contemplating real estate development, but I had some degree of uncertainty on how to transition. I suggested to Ronna, "Maybe I should build a couple of houses while we're starting to develop."

Ronna gazed at me with a familiar radiant smile and serene gray eyes. "Chuck, we just heard the service," she reminded. "Our pastor said, 'When one door closes, another door opens.' Let's close that door and open the next one," she suggested, resting her soft hand on mine.

I nodded in agreement. "Okay, let's take that leap of faith."

We did, and it turned out to be the best thing ever. If I hadn't been fully invested, I might not be as successful as I am today. With the support and encouragement of my wife, Ronna, I was ready and willing to take the chance.

Success takes a lot of focus, and being focused can help you achieve wealth. But just because you have a career that you're focused on doesn't mean it's the right one. Sometimes you fail because you aren't cut out to do that particular job or you are unwilling to put in the effort. If everything was easy, everyone would do it. I'm not the best swimmer, and if I competed, it would be an epic failure. One summer, I took a job as a painter, and it didn't take long for me to find that painting wasn't for me either. I was bored, didn't get satisfaction out of it, and wasn't good at cutting the lines with a paintbrush. I am a Type A personality, and when I couldn't cut the lines right, it frustrated the hell out of me. Some people find painting relaxing and enjoy it, but I didn't—so I moved on. If what you are doing *is* your thing, put everything you have into it. If it isn't, put everything you have into something else.

I didn't get into development to get rich. I got into it because I really liked it. Find out where your strengths lie, what you're passionate about, and do that. Success isn't about making money. People have said, "That's easy to say because you're wealthy." But I didn't do it to make money. *I didn't have money or come from wealth when I began. I built it from the ground up.*

I think anyone who really knew me would have assumed I'd go into some type of business, and they were right, except I had this innate desire to *build* my own. Money wasn't my focus—it was being successful. If I were successful, money would be the byproduct, and I understood my reputation would have a lot to do with success.

Why did I choose real estate? It is where my experience, passion, interest, and drive had taken me. The opportunities in real estate were not limited, and I was able to use my creativity.

Real estate is one of the top wealth-growing industries, along with technology, oil and gas, textiles, and finance. On the *Forbes* list, there are more billionaires in those five categories than anything else. Real estate is one of the easiest to learn about and grow wealth. It is a great investment.

The earth is covered in real estate. Most people want to own it, and I wanted in. I knew real estate was for sale and for lease. After I got my broker's license, I started driving around town with a yellow notepad and pen on the passenger seat. I called every single sign related to property that I could find, and then I tried to match the person selling with the one searching. I had a good understanding of the market, and I made enough calls that I generated the business I was looking for.

"What do you want for the property?" I'd ask. The person would tell me, and I'd call the number on another person's sign and ask, "What are you looking for?" If the response was, "I'm looking for a restaurant pad," or something else, I'd reply, "I have one." I'd send them a professional marketing package and then promptly follow up. Bringing together a buyer and seller taught me the value of real estate. For a year and a half, I made commissions while being educated. All the different educational things I learned were instrumental in my progress. Although I still have my broker's license, in the real estate development business, a license isn't required. However, the licenses I received contributed to my success in this business. Why? It's all relative—it's all knowledge.

In 1998, Eckerd Drugs was building freestanding structures when the pharmacy chain decided they didn't want to be in strip centers anymore. They wanted their own identity. The other major drugstores, Walgreens and CVS, were going freestanding too, and they competed to get the best corners and locations. It became the drugstore wars. I had a deal I'd put together, and I'd met another guy, Lee, who had put together a deal. Since we were going after the same business, we decided to go to Eckerd, present both deals, and see if we could land the account jointly. When we reached out to them, Eckerd asked, "Do you all have anything you can send?" We didn't have anything specifically for that particular business deal, but we put a formal presentation together, submitted it to them, and pursued another opportunity in the meantime. Eckerd let us know they liked the two sites that we had proposed, and we got the deal. We even found a third location. Based on the quality of our work, they offered us more opportunities. Lee and I agreed to become business partners, and Unicorp National Developments was born, again, purely on a handshake.

Lee and I rented a three-bedroom apartment and used it as our office space; initially, we couldn't afford an office, but that was soon to change. The problem Lee and I had was that neither of us was skilled in accounting; therefore, we wanted someone who could properly manage the bookkeeping. We decided the first key employee we'd hire would be a bookkeeper, as long as they'd also answer the phones, because we didn't have anyone to do that either. As our business continued growing, we hired more and more people. Before long, we had more business than we knew what to do with. *If you want to do well in business, you need a good attorney, banker, and accountant.*

One thing that helped us build Unicorp was creating an identity and name recognition by promoting the company. In the very beginning, we hired a marketing company before we even had a product. It was important to market the name and who we were. We gained interest in our company because people were curious. We wrapped a band around the *Orlando Business Journal* with our logo on it. The public was able to identify our logo before we had anything to speak of. Originally, our logo was the griffin, but years later, we decided that we needed something more corporate. Marketing Unicorp properly and creatively was crucial in helping us attract more business.

Freestanding drugstores were becoming the big thing. Eckerd received a call from Mr. Florenz Ourisman, who said, "I want to buy some drugstores." It was our first month in business as

Unicorp, and our name was given to Mr. Ourisman to contact as a developer. He did what Eckerd recommended and called us.

"I hear you're doing three drugstores," he said.

"Yes, we are," I replied.

"I want to buy them. I'm coming to Orlando and I want to meet with you," he insisted.

When he came in, my partner and I took him to see all three locations.

"Okay, I'm buying all of them right now," he announced without any hesitation.

We were just pouring the slabs of concrete. Offering full disclosure, I told him, "We haven't built them yet."

He said, "I'll close, pay off your land, pay you your profit, and put the money in the bank to build them. But I want to close now."

"Okay," I responded enthusiastically. After the meeting, the first call I made was to my wife. I said, "Honey, we just made four and a half million dollars." We were splitting it with my partner, but we literally accomplished that our first month of being in business. We reinvested that money and started doing more and more drugstores. My partner and I went on to build 90 drugstores together. I've exceeded 120 to date.

Walgreens, CVS, and Eckerd were competitors. When Eckerd sold, CVS bought them. Knowing there would be opportunities to develop additional drugstores, I didn't waste any time. I got on the phone and scheduled two meetings. The first was in Rhode Island. I flew there and met with the president of real estate for CVS.

I said, "I understand that you bought Eckerd. We've done a lot of Eckerd stores, and we would like to continue on with CVS."

His response was short and direct, "Why do we need you? We have our own people, and you were our competitor."

I wasn't discouraged because he was right. They did have their own developers, and we had been their competitor, but he didn't know how good we were. We got back on the plane with our track record and integrity and headed to the next meeting.

The second meeting was the following day with Walgreens. When we arrived, we met with their president of real estate. We knew what we were capable of providing for Walgreens, and we again were confident in our communication. We told him, "We built a bunch of Eckerds. As you know, they sold to CVS, and now we would like to build Walgreens."

He nodded his head and replied, "You know, we're trying to expand our company, and we need people like you. We would love to have you work with us and help us grow." It was a complete dichotomy of the two companies. While CVS said, "We don't want to deal with you," Walgreens said, "Welcome aboard." They wanted developers like us on their team. If someone told me no, I was certain there was a yes waiting for me elsewhere.

Unicorp has built drugstores for over twenty years, in Florida, Texas, Mississippi, Arizona, New York, Maryland, and Washington, DC. As we've grown, Unicorp has developed properties in twenty-six states. We go where there's opportunity.

We put the real estate under contract, designed the buildings, acquired the permits for them, and hired contractors to build them for us. Committed to providing our clients with the best, we did our due diligence and hired consultants who were experts in their fields. We wanted people who didn't need to be told how to do their job. We went to work, sold completed developments, and reinvested the capital. Some developments we kept for cash flow. *Notice that we reinvest often. It's how we grow.* Generally, I don't like selling anything—I wanted to keep everything because we worked to build impressive properties that we can take pride in. But if I kept everything, I wouldn't have the capital to expand. Although artists sell their paintings, it doesn't mean it's not *their* work of art. A da Vinci is still a da Vinci regardless of who owns it. I look at my developments that way.

The first *big* center we did was in 2001. We wanted to build a town center that cost a little over $20 million, but we needed to raise $5 million of capital to do it. I had a lot of friends in a strong network I had built over the years. I went to them and asked, "Hey, do you know someone who has money that may want to invest in a real estate deal?"

You never know who will respond to you, and you may be surprised, but if you don't take the initiative to *ask*, the answer will be *no one*. If you talk to people and ask around enough, you will find someone with money. It's hard to get money from institutions when you're young in business because you don't have a proven track record. You have to get someone to believe in you as much as you believe in yourself.

I was introduced to a guy who was interested in the opportunity. My reputation and integrity went into that meeting before I did. The outcome was that I showed him a good business plan, and he agreed to invest with me. He put up the capital, and we verbally agreed to split the profits evenly. Completing the project was quite fun. Years later, he ended up making more than double his investment. That investment was in our first significant center, The Fountains at Bay Hill. It was a beautiful, upscale retail center in Orlando, inside Arnold Palmer's Bay Hill community. It was always fully leased, because it was a place where people wanted to go; the design alone would grab anyone's attention. When you do impressive work, people will talk about it, and your reputation will attract more of what you want. Shortly after, Disney presented the opportunity to build Water Tower Place on their property in Celebration, Florida. It was a $40 million project with a miscellaneous retail center, a grocery store, casual dining, and a mixed-use development. We've learned over the years that when you create opportunities to bring the community together in a "live, work, and play" environment, you have concocted the recipe for success.

Once you develop a proven history, you can go to larger financial institutions anticipating a favorable outcome. Now, I can go to institutions such as Goldman Sachs, Citibank, and JPMorgan Chase and borrow against my past. In the beginning, you have to borrow against your business plan, character, and integrity.

The 9/11 attacks occurred the same year we developed The Fountains at Bay Hill. My partner and I went to New York just ten days after 9/11. As we made our way down to the financial district, there were no words spoken between us. The somber expressions, grief-stricken faces, and despair were inescapable—as was the presence of bravery. I walked through the remnants that terrorists left at our feet, finding it difficult to consciously breathe the air knowing what it was comprised of. The soot was inches thick—the ashes—human remains.

We came across a fence with a multitude of yellow ribbons tightly fastened to it. It was surreal. A teenage girl in jeans and a light blue jacket, with her brunette hair pulled back off of her drawn face, looked as if she'd been wandering the streets, searching for someone since the attacks. She stopped a few people ahead of us, spoke with them, and then approached us beseechingly. "I'm looking for my dad. Do you know who my dad is?" I could only shake my head.

The buildings were still burning. The financial district had collapsed. It was difficult to be there.

Ronna and I had our beautiful daughter, Riley, in November, and I wanted to be home with my family as much as possible. The media indicated that travel on commercial flights was going to be difficult, and we didn't know how long that would last. My wife and I were sitting at a McDonald's discussing my impending travel and the probability of cancellations and delays, given that I was developing drugstores all over the country. She suggested, "I think you need to buy a plane," and I agreed. It was time. Having a plane would allow me to conduct business and return home more efficiently.

Due to economic demand, one after another, opportunities continued to emerge. The Pritzker family, who owns the Hyatt hotel chain, recognized that we were doing quality projects and wanted to do business with us. They bought the Orlando naval base that had closed under the Clinton administration. We bought fifty-six acres from them in the center of the base and built the Baldwin Park Town Center, another stunning mixed-use development. The impressive property became an organic attraction for people. In 2007, Baldwin Park sold for $100 million.

Unicorp was on quite a roll in 2007, and we had experienced an extended period of growth, but it took a lot of work. Lee and I were on our Bombardier Learjet heading to New York when I took a moment to observe my surroundings. I sat back for a moment and contemplated the amount of hard work and personal sacrifice it had taken to purchase a luxury aircraft of that magnitude. I considered how often we used the aircraft for business and the effort it took to be successful. Then I broke the silence and stated, "You really don't want to work like I want to work."

Lee gave a brief moment of reflection and confessed, "Chuck, I'm at the age in my life where I don't want to work hard. I kind of want to retire. When you get to my age, you will want to do the same."

After a ten-year partnership, Unicorp was very profitable, but I realized that we were steadily taking two vastly different paths. Lee and I knew what our portfolio was worth, so I made him a generous offer. I told him he could be a silent partner; I would do all the work and retain the majority of the profits. Lee turned his head slightly and gazed out the oval window into the drifting pillows of clouds. When he returned his attention, he released a slight grin and demurred. "I would rather just be bought out."

After our discussion, we agreed to a significant buyout in the tens of millions. We sat on the plane and wrote the agreed-upon terms on two pieces of paper. After review, we both signed it. A few months later, Lee and I were sitting on my back porch by the lake. We had a stack of paperwork on the table in front of us. Silence occupied the space between us as I imagined what this change would mean.

I said, "Lee, I don't know who's making the best deal here, you or me. I could easily switch places with you and take that buyout, but you know what? It's what we agreed to do, what I want to do, and what you want to do. I wish you the best in life." We signed the legal paperwork, I handed him a check, signifying the dissolution of our partnership. I was the sole owner of Unicorp National Developments.

Make the determination that you want to be a winner and then succeed. There are many winners in business and in many fields, but it is a cognitive decision you make. Every day you wake up, you have to look at yourself and determine, "I will succeed. I am a winner." If you don't instill this self-confidence, you will settle on mediocrity.

—CHUCK WHITTALL

Chapter 4

Rebuilding After the Great Recession

At some point in life, everyone questions whether they can persevere through adversity, but it's possible, if they choose to be optimistic. I thought about what I endured during my childhood, not because I couldn't get past what happened to me, but because I could, and I did. I wasn't meant to adopt a negative mentality for the rest of my life; that period of time was just the beginning. It was helping me decide who and what I wanted to be. I felt incredibly uncomfortable and was often reminded that I didn't fit into that environment, but I knew I wouldn't remain in that position. It made me find a way to fix what I didn't like rather than complain about it. I couldn't change others, but I did possess the propensity to change my circumstances as well as myself. I tend to see the positive side of things, and that mindset makes me happy. If I don't obtain a project that I want, it's unfortunate, but perhaps I wasn't supposed to get that one. I accept it and move on. But of course, that is after putting in the necessary effort to acquire it.

There are many components to help you progress, yet optimism is one that helps to solve problems and move you forward where ubiquitous opportunities are waiting. You're not meant to fight everything. Optimism creates a different mindset to find another way to accomplish a goal versus a negative person who hits a roadblock and stops. You will find a way to open a door rather than close it. Always knowing there is a way kept me moving forward when there were barriers so big I couldn't see over them.

———⋯———

After reinvesting my profits from the Baldwin Park deal to buy out my partner, I was ready to move on to my next project. I flew to Richmond, Virginia, and built West Broad Village for a half-billion dollars without any partners. I was focused on growing the company. I had an incredible team at Unicorp, and we were doing super well. We were working on several developments, we had properties that we held with great tenants, and there was more on the horizon. Then—*boom!* The rug was pulled out from under us when the market collapsed and the Great Recession occurred in 2008. Everything stopped. The silence and darkness injected a considerable dose of fear into the masses. I'd gone from closing a deal practically every week to not closing any deals. We were facing a global economic downturn that devastated the world financial markets as well as the banking and real estate industries. I was being tested on a level I'd never imagined, and *uncomfortable* was an understatement.

After the collapse of Lehman Brothers, the largest bankruptcy in history, it was a struggle for survival. It would have been believable that practically everyone in the world was affected by the financial crisis. There were increases in mortgage foreclosures, millions of people lost their savings, jobs, and homes—they were gone. Unemployment was high. Households made changes in the way they operated. I learned that women would not get their hair cut or done every four weeks; they did so every six weeks. As a result, the salon business dropped 30 to 40 percent. People cleaned their own swimming pools, which meant the pool companies weren't making money. Restaurants weren't doing well because people weren't eating out. Nearly everyone was affected in some capacity, and if we wanted to survive, we had to pull back, readjust, and work with all our tenants and banks.

Unicorp survived the Great Recession by having a lot of conversations. We knew if the banks wanted to, they could lower the hammer at any time and end everything I was fighting to sustain. One of my bankers with CIBC World Markets, Barrie Wood, advised, "Chuck, as long as you continue to add value, and the bank realizes you're adding value, we will continue to work together." I never forgot that. I wanted to make sure the banks knew I was valuable and that they were better off with me than without me. I got up and went to work early every day to prove myself to them regardless of the pressure I was under. The landscape had changed, and banks were in the business of taking properties back. I didn't want any of ours to be on the list.

It wasn't a secret that the environment had become increasingly problematic for a lot of people, but rather than face those issues head-on, people ran from them. I did the opposite and ran toward them. When I was having issues with our properties, I let the banks know what the problems were and how we were handling them. I did everything possible to maintain transparency. Had I stopped taking their phone calls, they would have engaged their attorneys and problems would have come down the pipe. Although it was a horrible market and some of our tenants couldn't pay their rent, I let the banks know we were doing everything we could do, and they couldn't do better than what we were doing.

During the recession, there were limited buyers, except for bottom feeders who wanted to buy property for next to nothing. There were few liquidity events, and the banks were extremely cautious, making it difficult to invest in real estate.

Financially, my personal life was stable, but stress was part of the atmosphere. Ronna and I were able to do the things we always had, but she and Riley became the inspiration for me to survive the Great Recession. We still had our health, our home, the airplane, and other things, but the mental stress was tremendous. The fear of losing everything was always looming. The duration of the recession was incalculable, as it could only correct itself. I had no other recourse than to remain optimistic and continue removing barriers one by one. I wish I'd had more faith at the time, but the market was collapsing, and we didn't know where the floor was. While the Great Recession engulfed one business after another, we did everything we could not to be one of them.

On those bad days, you have to keep functioning as if they are good days. Even during a recession, you have to pick yourself up by the bootstraps, go to work, and function. The key is to continue doing things to move forward, even if the movement is slow. You can't let it get to you. I kept working and finding solutions because, as difficult as times were, I never doubted the outcome for Unicorp. It was possible for us to survive—we just had to fight. It was the uncertainty of the recession's duration that was taxing.

One objective should be to focus on performance so that you stay on track and are able to measure your progress. The way life works is that you are either in the storm or there is a storm ahead. Money doesn't make you exempt from problems, and life isn't perfect for everyone all the time. Sometimes the only thing to do is not give up.

There were numerous changes transpiring, and people were waiting to see who was going out of business. I let some employees go, cut the pay of all my remaining employees by 20 percent, and then gave them Fridays off to try and compensate. I wasn't asking them to work for a discount because that would not have been fair to them. Watching the majority of my team come in on Fridays, displaying their commitment to the success of Unicorp, was extremely humbling. Unfortunately, trimming back was necessary to pay the bills and survive—we were fighting to keep our doors open and persevere. It was hard. In that economy, no one had faith in anyone. We worked diligently to handle problems while trying to alleviate the question of survival. Many of my contemporaries lost their business in one of the hardest times in history for people.

———•———

Going to work every day without knowing when things would turn around was frustrating. I couldn't tell Ronna when things would return to normal, and I was working even harder to make sure they would. We'd get on the phone and call lenders to ask if they were open for business, and they'd all say no. We couldn't look for new development projects until the lenders opened their doors for business. We, too, were at the mercy of the market.

One of the hardest things was not feeling in control of my destiny. When I made a poor decision, I owned it; however, this time I was vulnerable and reacting to world events that were beyond my control. We did our best navigating through the devastation, since we had no power over stopping it. Our only objective was surviving.

I needed a new CFO at Unicorp, and I thought about a guy, Dale Fitch, whom I'd met over dinner with mutual friends. Dale was in the 82nd Airborne Division of the United States Army. He was working for someone else when we met, but there was something about his character and overall communication that I respected. He was one of those guys you meet and instinctively know you can trust. On July 6, 2010, I called Dale because I wanted him on my team—and it turned out to be the right call.

"Hey, you worked in real estate—in accounting?"

"Yes."

"I'm looking for a CFO. Are you interested in discussing the opportunity?"

"Yes, I'd be interested, but can I call you after I'm done working?" he asked.

Dale came in and interviewed for an hour and a half, though we negotiated his contract via text. The first day Dale came into the office, he was already an employee. The inaugural meeting I took him to was a special assets meeting with the bankers, who were constantly disgruntled at the time. I wanted him to dive in, and when he did, it felt like we had been working together for years.

I told Dale, "It's good that you're coming in now, because in six months or when things turn around, you will have experienced enough of the pain so you'll understand it. When things get better, you will appreciate what we went through."

Dale said, "Let me handle everything inside the office to give you the ability to go out and do what you do well—get business."

The six-month time frame exceeded two years. I continued to let people do what they did best, and Dale did a great job of freeing up my time. I'm often looking at the same side of the moon—the bright, positive side, and I'd often tell Dale, "Quit being negative."

He typically would reply, "I'm just looking out for the other side."

Dale made me pay attention to the other side, and he brought balance to our work environment. And when needed, he'd reel me in a little bit.

———

One of the rules in my business is "Don't fall in love with real estate," but I did. I owned my office, and I didn't want to sell it. I created a beautiful property, and I was in love with it, but with the recession, there were things I had to get off my balance sheet. I couldn't borrow money, and the banks were saying, "Your loan matured. You have to pay us off." Some projects were like babies to me, and I didn't want to sell them, but doing so was the best decision we ever made.

On October 19, 2012, which happens to be Ronna's birthday, our capital event—selling six properties, including Dellagio and Bay Hill Fountains, for $263 million—was significant enough to make the *Wall Street Journal*, *Bloomberg*, and other major financial papers. It made people more familiar and comfortable with Unicorp. Perception goes a long way, and in that economy, the general view was that developers wouldn't survive. That influx of capital from selling assets opened the door for us to do more business and gave us room to breathe.

The next day, I was back in the office at 8:00 a.m., ready to move forward. We had stabilized our company. Clearing so much debt off my balance sheet created a substantial cash influx, and we became bankable again. I redeployed the cash and had the money to do deals. That was the stake in the ground to our banks and the marketplace, showing we were surviving. Unicorp was going to be around.

The effects of the Great Recession were so profound that the big turnaround for Unicorp didn't happen until 2013. At the point the market took off, there wasn't the same amount of competition exiting the recession. For those who survived, there was a wealth of opportunity on the other side.

In real estate development, nothing is too big or too small. The first real estate deal I ever did was for $13,000, and I was only twenty-one years old. Ronna and I had bought a foreclosed home, fixed it up, and sold it. After making a good profit, we reinvested it into more foreclosed homes and flipping houses. I started at the bottom and came to appreciate and understand the need to have incremental growth patterns. Now, I am doing deals in the hundreds of millions.

When you are starting out in real estate development, don't ever consider any deal as being too small. If you are determined not to fail, you must work to become proficient in all areas of your chosen field—communications, negotiations, networking, sales, and other areas. And then make the investment and take the time to understand all aspects of real estate development or your business in general.

Meeting Michael Jackson when I was a disc jockey, the same week Thriller debuted.

My Passion—Driving with the Ferrari team.

Prepping for a race.

Dellagio—When Development Is Art

Watertower Place—My First Project with Disney

Dellagio—Inspired by Bellagio

The Fountains—My First Big Development

Celebration—Opening Doors

The Wheel, an Orlando Icon—Proud to bring this to Orlando.

Vacationing in Bora Bora—What could be more beautiful?

Bora Bora—Balance of work and play.

Travel—I have been lucky to travel the world and love Europe.

Making Memories—Watching my little girl grow up.

Riley's Homecoming—I flew back from Texas to surprise her. Wouldn't miss it for the world.

In a challenge, you will either be a winner or loser. When I think of a challenge, I am never willing to lose. That's why I look at things not as challenges but as obstacles, and figure out a different way to accomplish my goal or mission.

—CHUCK WHITTALL

Chapter 5

A Reflection on My Experience

In my twenties, I was in the process of determining what I wanted to do, but in my thirties and forties, I was learning and perfecting my profession. I even thought my most profitable years were my forties—until now. I believe they are my fifties. I've gained so much wisdom from my thirties and forties that I am currently running on all cylinders, and it's great. I feel that I really know what I'm doing, and I've learned how to do it right through experiences that have helped cultivate better judgment, decision-making, patience, tolerance, humility, faith, and optimism. A reflection on my experience and what I have learned equates to wisdom.

Opportunities derive from treating people well and doing what's right, even in the worst of times when it may seem the hardest thing to do. Buying out my partner cost tens of millions, and it was washed down with the Great Recession. But the chaser was still optimism, and it was much needed because I had a great deal of work ahead of me.

The recession was over, and it was time to move past what was lost, get back to building, and continue moving forward void of anger or bitterness. I had to draw on my experiences and life lessons so that we could creatively surpass everything we'd already done. The business was there; however, we had to remove the rubble to find it. You may not have what you want at a specific moment, but if you bust your ass, you are going to move up or change your circumstances. Whatever job you do or career you carve out, do it to the best of your ability and do it passionately, especially in the worst of times; *it will help you ascend.*

Everyone who survived seemed to flush out of the Great Recession at the same time. Unicorp hadn't borrowed for a few years, and 2013 presented signs of opportunities. The first indication was that we were able to get a loan and start doing business again. Our first deal went well. We paid off more debt and reinvested in new deals. What got us rolling were the drugstores, apartment buildings, and the mere fact that I didn't have financial partners. Business took off, and from there, we started to explode.

We lost many of our peers, and there weren't a lot of developers out there who were able to perform. After the recession, some of them didn't have the capital. Fortunately, we didn't have to go to financial investment institutions or solicit external funding from investors to be our capital partners, and that helped us grow. We consistently reinvested our own capital and continued to expand into apartments, town centers, mixed-use centers, and hotels. I told people that Unicorp was also a real estate investment company. We considered options from residential to commercial, mixed-use, and hotels, and invested in top-tier real estate deals.

Managing finances is one of the most significant parts of what I do, which is the reason I pay attention to rates. To many, 1 percent doesn't sound like a lot; however, a 1 percent move in the market equates to big dollars. I'm not exclusively in the development business. I am in the construction, sales and leasing, and finance business. *When you are an entrepreneur, it's best to learn as much as possible, study so you can master your craft, and follow the trends to fully comprehend your industry and all that it takes to be successful.*

Before the Great Recession, I bought a property that was in bankruptcy for tens of millions. The property had a partially operational mall on it. Since it was about to become a development that exceeded $100 million, I paid the tenants to vacate the property so we could tear it down. Knowingly, I was getting rid of that income stream, with plans to create a new one.

I had just returned to the States when the market collapsed. My banker in New York, Barrie Wood, who held the loan on that property, called, insisting that I go to New York. Things were already chaotic, but this was a priority. Given the economy and his urgency to meet in person, I was sure he had unfavorable news. I agreed and flew to New York the following day. When I walked into Barrie's office, I realized I was right. Barrie and I had a good relationship, but I sensed his discomfort in the way he greeted me. As we entered his posh conference room, he grabbed the handles on both of the massive glass doors, closing them behind him, as if it had been rehearsed. He'd never done that before in all the meetings I'd had in that room. I inhaled, took in the view of the New York skyline, and exhaled as he motioned for me to have a seat.

In a grave tone, Barrie stated, "We need to talk."

I sat down, threw up my hands and said, "Well, I'm here."

The silence was deafening.

He took a deep breath and said, "With this Lehman collapse, the financial market is having a meltdown. Chuck, we can't move forward on your loan. With the spreads in the market—the finance rates are blown out."

I sighed. "What do you suggest?"

He shrugged and alleged, "We think it'll rebound soon. Let's wait a month or so, and then we should be able to do it."

"That's fine. We can wait," I said placidly.

Until we reconvened, I still had to make the payments each month on the $35 million balance I owed on that loan. The dejection in Barrie's eyes told me he wasn't sure how long it would take. How could he? No one knew how big this thing was. In the interim, I returned home and waited like everyone else. My banker's month or two turned into five years.

When we were finally able to develop that property, we began building Orlando's ICON Park in 2013, which took two years to complete. The grand opening was in May 2015, and business was booming. The Wheel at ICON Park was a big deal. It was a turning point for getting out of debt, for the Central Florida market and for the market in general. It was truly an iconic sign that we had exited the recession. Included in the development were Madame Tussauds and Sea Life Aquarium on the property as tenants. We turned that property around and brought a new level of excitement to Orlando.

Ronna, Riley, and I often vacationed along Florida's central west coast, in Longboat Key, and we loved it. In 2013, Ronna and I discussed buying a piece of property there to build eight townhomes, along with a clubhouse. The idea was to sell them to our close friends, so we could all hang out with our families and have fun. However, the property we were interested in was sold to someone else, and we couldn't make that happen, but I had options; there was more real estate to explore. I drove up and down Longboat Key, taking in more than I ever had, and discovered a beautiful beachfront property on 17.3 acres that sat right on the Gulf of Mexico. The view was phenomenal. Although the historic property was abandoned and dilapidated, I envisioned what it could be—an extraordinary property with incredible potential.

The property was the Colony Beach and Tennis Resort. The Colony came with a fascinating and rich history that has left many with treasured memories. At one point, it was regarded as the most famous tennis resort in the world. It's where Nick Bollettieri taught Andre Agassi how to play tennis. Audrey Hepburn and a host of other celebrities vacationed there, and it was reported that George W. Bush spent the night there and woke up on the morning of the 9/11 attacks. Respectfully, I believed that the narrative of the Colony was too incredible to revive, but that location had long awaited something innovative and spectacular in its place that would honor it by disclosing memories of what once had been.

April 14, 2013, was the final day of the Masters Tournament in Augusta, Georgia. I was walking down the breathtaking stretch of the back nine comprising the iconic Amen Corner. I always thought it was important to recognize fashion, considering that it reflects character the same way our choices do. That day, I caught sight of a lady ten feet in front of me wearing a brightly colored floral-print dress, also following the crowd. I darted up next to her and blurted, "I see you're all dressed in Lilly. You must be so sad that Lilly Pulitzer died last week."

Composedly placing her hand on her chest, she professed, "Yes, Lilly was my hero. I just love Lilly." As if she were reflecting on a specific memory, she slowly slid her hand across her dress. "I'm wearing Lilly to honor her today."

I nodded to acknowledge her thoughtfulness and turned to address the gentlemen walking alongside her. I asked, "So where are you from?"

"We're from Florida," he replied.

"Me, too. What part?"

"Sarasota."

"Really? We vacation in Sarasota. There's a piece of property in Sarasota I would love to buy."

"What property?" the gentleman asked inquisitively.

"It's the Colony. The famed resort that sits right on the Gulf."

"Well, I'm the bankruptcy attorney, Morgan Bentley," he said, extending his hand.

"Really?" I shook his hand, introduced myself, and asked, "How do I buy it?"

He reached in his pocket and said, "Let me give you my card. Why don't you give me a call tomorrow?"

"I will. Enjoy the tournament," I added, placing his business card in my wallet.

The next day, I called Morgan, and he said, "If you want to buy the Colony, there are a few things you need to know."

"I'm listening."

"It's mired down in litigation," he warned. "There are tons of lawsuits—foreclosures and bankruptcies. It's a mess."

"Okay. What's the first step?" I asked.

He provided a list of phone numbers, and I began making the calls as soon as I hung up. A couple of days later, I went to see the property again. After standing there for a few minutes admiring the view while reflecting on the history, I said to myself, *If someone is going to do this, it may as well be me. If someone else does it, it's because I didn't do it.* If I didn't chase after this opportunity and then someday drove by the resort to find that someone else had developed it, it would signify that I had given up. I took in a deep breath of fresh air and closed my eyes for a brief moment. I wasn't going to let this slip away. Besides, it just felt right, as though it were my time. I exhaled and committed to getting Longboat Key done, but we encountered a big problem—a puzzle unlike any other.

Morgan Bentley was right about everything he said. The Colony was a giant ball of knotted twine. I've been cleaning up the mess, and it's taken eight years, but we're almost completely finished with everything. We've solved nearly all of the litigation on the property and have invested tens of millions into putting a St. Regis Hotel there.

For years, the town said the Colony wouldn't get done, and understandably so; it hasn't been an easy feat. I remember when I walked into the town manager's office for the first time, and after speaking with him, he explained, "Many developers have come in my office and said they were going to get this done, but for some reason, I think you're the guy who is really going to do it."

When I want to do something, my team and I will do whatever is necessary to find a way to accomplish that objective. Relationships and the way we treat people can open doors and offer assistance in ways we didn't imagine. Initiating a pleasant conversation with strangers led me to meet and work with the bankruptcy attorney of the Colony. Communication and making connections are such important skills. You never know what will come of paying attention to the way one is dressed or the way you dress.

Make sure to embrace the good habits and skills that are beneficial to your overall development. Being a DJ opened the door for me to be more outgoing and communicative. Your experiences can help you evolve in business if you let them. Own them and use them. I have had years of organic networking, and I love meeting new and interesting people. It's how we learn and grow—even in real estate.

I've met numerous people in the development business. I travel and interact with people regularly, and I never know whom I will cross paths with or end up doing business with. The key is that regardless of the opportunity, always do the right thing, or don't do it at all. You can build great friendships by taking the time to converse with people. You can create outstanding professional relationships and garner referrals, but when you do what is right, it feels good.

In 2016, I met Michael Jordan due to a potential opportunity with Unicorp. Michael had driven up from Jupiter, Florida, to meet with his son Marcus, me, and my leasing director. We met at the ICON because Marcus was interested in renting space for his shoe store, the Trophy Room. Like many others, I had watched Michael throughout his career. He was always the best, hardworking, and extremely driven. Engaging with Michael Jordan in regard to a potential business deal shed light on other sides of him—father and businessman. When we walked the space, Michael communicated his questions and concerns about his son's business, and he had plenty. Here was a billionaire who could have given his son a check for any amount of money and not blink an eye, but he cared about the particulars.

After viewing the space and discussing the details, Michael turned to me, looked directly in my eyes, and asked one final question, "Chuck, will my son's business be successful here?"

I responded, "Michael, I'd love to have your son as a tenant, but to be honest, I don't think this is the right location for him. I think you should put it someplace else because we're not really retail here. We're more experiential."

Michael nodded appreciatively.

I could have said yes, just to have Michael Jordan's son as a tenant; however, we don't want people to fail. We want to look out for the interests of others. If our tenants are successful, we are successful.

Michael and Marcus appreciated our honesty and ended up putting the business in downtown Disney Springs. Our team came over to the Orlando ICON, and Michael was gracious enough to take pictures with them. He was very nice, but what struck me was that he drove two and a half hours to see the space and ensure his son was making a solid decision. Michael's leadership extended far beyond the basketball court.

While the success of others is paramount to us, there may be tenants who will go through challenging times; since you don't control *their* business, they can take you with them. Things happen—but you won't come out of those situations too well by being angry. Be slow to anger, because things are going to happen that are beyond your control, and the solution isn't found inside an angry mindset.

In the real estate development business, there have been mistakes that have cost us *millions*. Any time anyone brings me a problem, I never look at it to see who I'll yell or scream at; instead, I ask, "How do we fix it? What do we need to do?" or I'll say, "Let's figure out how we're going to solve this." Regardless of how bad the problem is, there's *always* a viable solution. Dale often reminds me, *You don't look to the past, you look to the future.*

We were selling a great piece of property that we had owned for five years. Everything had gone smoothly with it; the tenants were great. Unicorp received an aggressive offer on the property for $63 million, and we decided to accept it. There was a thirty-day inspection period, and we were closing fifteen days later, which was a short window of time. During the thirty days, we had two tenants fall out of business, and we suggested to the potential buyer that we would master lease by paying the rent on the space until we found new tenants. The buyer approved of moving forward. We were supposed to go hard on the transaction a week later, which meant it was nonrefundable, and the buyer was committed to close. Then, one of our substantial tenants, who occupied 10 percent of the space, didn't pay us rent either. On the twelfth of the month, the buyer sent an email stating that they needed to review our accounts receivable ledger for that property. They wanted verification that all of our tenants had paid their rent. We sent the ledger and they responded, noting the other tenant who had yet to pay us.

Sounding frustrated, they questioned, "When is that tenant paying their rent?"

I was concerned that the buyer wouldn't go hard on the transaction because the tenant hadn't paid. We knew the tenant was having some financial struggles, so I called the CEO, and he blatantly acknowledged, "Chuck, we don't have any money. We're going broke. We can't pay rent."

The tenant literally could cost me $63 million because he hadn't paid his $30,000 rent. At the end of the conversation, the tenant replied, "Sorry. We can't do anything."

I sent an email to my buyer and told him we needed to get on the phone. We had a conference call that afternoon, and I was transparent, as there was no reason to make excuses. "They're going out of business, and they aren't going to pay us. But it's a very desirable space, and we'll find another tenant quickly," I assured him.

"Chuck, we're not going hard," was all he said.

We were expecting to close on the sale the following week. In order to save the deal, I suggested, "I don't need long. Just let me work on it, and I'll get back to you."

You create a lot of your own destiny by the choices you make. But what accompanied a great choice was having complete confidence in my team. I went to my leasing team and said, "You've got to go find a new tenant." And they did.

On Thursday of that week, a restaurant out of California was looking at the space, and they let us know they wanted it. We wrote a letter of intent and sent it to them on Friday. By Saturday morning, we had a signed deal.

Two days later, I said to Dale, "What a difference a day makes." Everything seemed horrible on Tuesday, and then we put it all back together. The buyer moved forward, and we made $700,000 more than what the initial transaction would have been.

I maintained the position that we would keep moving forward. Too often people act in the moment, because that moment seems so bad, irreparable, or calamitous. They don't realize that things can change quickly if you just give them a chance and let that next day come. Things can turn around and be okay again—in business and in your personal life. Reflect on your experiences and everything you've already overcome as a reminder of your ability to persevere. Were there times when you felt things were hopeless, yet you were able to turn them around? Be slow to anger, understanding that things are going to happen and challenges are inevitable. Have faith, be patient, and get to work.

When you are building relationships, refrain from taking advantage of others. That's not good business. Engaging in business that is mutually beneficial is good practice. You will come out of difficult times and make a resurgence stronger and better than ever by doing the right things—and we are given many opportunities to do so. Sunny days always follow rainy days.

The American Dream is not solely about starting your own business, it's also about becoming something more in business.

—CHUCK WHITTALL

Chapter 6

Building Wealth through Real Estate

For those who are working to acquire wealth, the common element is that they are hungry. The question then becomes: How much wealth do you want? Some say, "Enough to be comfortable," but your comfort levels change. The goalpost continues to move, and there is always going to be someone making more than you. But are you willing to fight for what you want? *Your level of hunger exemplifies your drive in life and contributes to the outcome.* Those who say they want to be successful have to work for it. If you're an athlete and you want to be highly rated, you show up, train, and practice with your team, and continue developing your skills on your own. Hunger is a deep desire. Your level of commitment reveals *how badly* you want it, and success depends on that commitment.

My childhood caused me to question where I was meant to be in life. When I made the determination that I wanted to be happy, successful, and able to take pride in my work, that inspired me to put everything I had into whatever I did. When I made the choice to get into real estate development, it felt right. I was fascinated by it and passionate about utilizing the knowledge I had gained. Making the transition into real estate helped me discover what I was meant to do. Real estate development didn't have a ceiling as to how good I could become or how far I could advance.

After completing a real estate development project, I have a moment that produces a sense of accomplishment—not only for myself, but for my team. Why is that? *Because we are rewarded by the work.* I don't wait for anyone to pat me on the back and say, "Great job, Chuck." I'm *supposed* to do a great job. *We* are supposed to do a great job. It's what our clients expect and what we demand of ourselves as a company. You are a confident individual when you do things the right way. You don't need approval because you've done the best you can. When I build something special and then sell it for a great deal of money, that means the buyer loved the end product. It's like art. If an artist paints something beautiful, they don't need someone to tell them it's beautiful, they just know. I am committed to doing anything I do to the best of my ability, and in some way I challenge myself to make each project better. You can, too, when you are continuously learning and expanding your skill set. The environment is ever-changing, and it is your responsibility to keep up or become obsolete.

When you start making a healthy income, your lifestyle changes and you start buying things that you've wanted. A bigger home or another vacation home. One car turns into two, and so on. You will buy more because you have more. But—money shouldn't be what makes you happy. You should be happy doing what brings you joy and comfort. This has always worked for me.

Some mornings, I wake up wishing I could be lazy and just stay in bed, but I can't. I don't have it in me. People who are successful start early. We know there have to be sacrifices, and those same sacrifices have taught me how to build wealth. Yet one thing I do is take time to recharge so that I don't become overwhelmed. Self-care is essential to your well-being, and your success is contingent upon your health—mental, physical, and emotional. Work hard, but get the appropriate amount of rest and establish balance in your life. The work will be there, but your health must be managed or the productivity won't.

Once you learn how to make a hundred dollars, you know how to make a hundred dollars. When you learn how to make a *million* dollars, you know how to make a million dollars. Working hard as an entrepreneur taught me how to make money, and if you've learned from it, your experience has taught you what to do and how. In summary, if I lost everything, as long as I had my health, I would find an investor who would handle the financial obligations. I would identify a great property to buy and develop. The next step would be to determine what we could charge and what we would do with the space. I would then sell that property. The investor would get half the profit and I would take my half— and by now, you know what I'd do. Invest it. By then, I would have accomplished my goal of making a million dollars. Now, I'm back on track. Giving up would not have been the answer, and it reminded me of a song. When I got knocked down, I got back up again, too. And you can do that—when you're healthy!

I've learned how to do my business well, and I have friends that can do the same thing, because they know the recipe for success. *Drive is instinctive.* The American Dream is that we can all do what we want in this country. If you want to be successful, put in the effort and continue to persevere—don't stop.

Approximately eighteen years ago, I was in the Delta Crown Room at the airport in Washington, DC, when I met a guy. We started talking, and I discovered that he was quite successful in his field of business. I was curious, so I asked *how* he'd become so successful.

He replied, "Have you ever seen a mouse in a maze with a piece of cheese at the other end? That mouse will go through the wall, over the wall, under the wall, and around the wall to do whatever it takes to get the cheese. Always remember—get the cheese," he advised.

That stayed with me. In fact, I would tell people that we've got to get the cheese, because there's always a solution. It may not be the best solution, but there is one if you look for it. When my daughter Riley has a question or problem, I tell her to figure it out. Why? I want Riley to be successful. To do so, you have to possess that attitude.

Servant leadership is how I operate. I empower people to make decisions, which is how people confidently learn to solve problems. My schedule is packed, I am involved with several different things, I am passionate about the charity work I do, and I have a family. Time is money, and micromanagement slows you down. In my line of business, I would rather attempt fifty things and make a mistake on one or two but still complete forty-eight of them well, versus doing twenty things perfectly, because we could have done so much more. Naturally, you will have occasions where the best decision isn't made, but if people give it their best effort and try hard, those decisions are forgivable and able to be overcome. This is especially true when they are used as learning opportunities. Regarding my team, I trust that they will come out with the best solution.

You can't build wealth if you are preoccupied with distractions that don't pertain directly to the primary objective. Micromanaging isn't power, it's a waste of time.

——•——

Another way to build wealth in real estate is by *finding a way forward*. There will always be barriers, controversy, or moments that you find yourself at an impasse. I've had occasions where I've gone into controversial meetings where we haven't agreed on something. It happens. But when I'm going into one of those meetings, I've learned to *use words that lead to a noncontroversial way forward*.

I was in Longboat Key, sitting at the table with three other gentlemen. They were butting heads about what I wanted to do. It appeared effortless for one of the gentlemen to insist, "No. We don't like what you're doing." We could have ended the conversation at that juncture without progress, but instead, since he didn't like my way, I simply asked one logical question to keep the discussion flowing.

"Okay," I began, gaining everyone's attention. "Show me a way forward. How would you like to see this progress?" All of a sudden, the energy changed, and we found ourselves talking more productively, and then, before you knew it, we were compromising. That's how you get to a solution. You don't want to arrive at a crossroads where it's your way or the highway. That's not a healthy or professional approach in business because it displays your unwillingness to compromise. You are more inclined to cause people to imitate your behavior, become obstinate, and then you lose. The art of negotiation is getting people to come your way without them realizing it.

When you reach a barrier, the best thing to do is ask, "How can we move forward?" I said that to bankers during the recession, and it helped the outcome and kept us advancing in the right direction. We all know what the problem is, but now *you* are asking *them* to help find a solution. That one question makes people think creatively, and it can keep the business on the table.

People miss out on opportunities that can help build wealth by coming to a standoff. I don't mind letting people see that I don't need to be the smartest guy in the room. I'd much rather be surrounded by intelligent people who give me productive ideas. That's how you grow. The knowledge of others has helped me solve problems, and people don't generally like problem-solving because it's uncomfortable. Sometimes it means you have to compromise, and I've had to do that a great deal. Things can't always be your way.

I have a development project called the City Center developments in Troy, Michigan. The first phase of the project was office and retail space, and the last phase was apartments. There were several legitimate issues that unfolded that amounted to a $7 million problem. It easily could have been a cut-and-dried situation I let my director of finance handle. Instead, I felt this was something that I needed to address with the contractor. There were tariffs raising steel costs, as well as generally escalating prices and a labor shortage because of low unemployment. Although I had a guaranteed contract with my contractor, these weren't issues that he could control or necessarily foresee. Things can sometimes negatively affect us in a good economy, and we have to be willing to reconfigure. Even though the apartments would cost more to build, the financial benefit is uncompromised because the economy is doing well.

When I walked in the conference room, I said, "Look, guys, I don't want you to take a position on why you think you are right on your side, and I'm not going to take that position on how I'm right on my side. Let's figure out how we can solve this problem together. Let's walk through it, understand it, and come up with a solution that works for everyone at this table." The energy in the room changed, and we sat there until that goal was accomplished.

I could have told the contractor, "You have a contract. Live up to it," but that wouldn't have been the right decision.

If you are going into any situation where there has to be a winner and loser, there will be many occasions where *you* will lose. When you seek a win-win and it works for both sides, then a greater percentage of the time you are not going to be a loser. That's my position with conflicts. Whenever you get in a situation, establish what you both agree on and work from there.

When we left, my director of finance, Larry, asked, "Why did you give in and negotiate? We have a contract."

"Larry, it would have hurt his business, and he wouldn't be able to finish our project. We had to work it out so that it's a win-win for both of us. If it cost more than expected, we just have to deal with that."

If we couldn't come to a resolution, most likely the contractor would walk off the job. We'd have to hire another contractor, and we would end up paying more money. In the end, it would have prolonged the project. Again, time is a valuable resource, and we have several other projects that require our time and focus. When you are able to achieve financial goals, that is a contribution to building wealth.

There are many occasions when people like and trust you. They bet on the jockey. They want to know your character and whom they are doing business with before they engage in a business transaction with you. It's not always about money; more often than you know, it's about you.

There was a deal we were trying to do in Daytona Beach. Years prior, I had read and listened to a motivational speech about ways to connect with whomever you are meeting with. It had an impact on me. I was working with one of my employees, Tim, who said, "Chuck, I can't break him. I can't get Cooper to sell the property. I'm scheduled to meet with him tomorrow, but I don't think I can pull this deal off," he confessed. "Will you go to the meeting with me?"

I agreed.

The following day, Tim took me to Cooper's office and introduced us. I didn't sit down right away. I walked around and looked at the pictures and mementos he had surrounding him. There were many that revealed Cooper was a hunter and a family man.

I started asking him questions about his photos. "This is a cool picture," I said pointing at a nicely framed photo on his wall. "Tell me about this one. Where were you?"

"Montana," Cooper replied proudly. "I was on a hunting trip with my boys…," and a healthy conversation was initiated. Tim smiled as he listened to the in-depth conversation and light banter being exchanged.

I spent the majority of our time connecting to what was important to Cooper instead of chasing after business from a stranger. If we got it, fine. If not, that was fine, too. But either way, I wanted to know more about the person I was interested in doing business with. The majority of his pictures had something to do with hunting, telling me *that* was his life.

Connecting with people or building rapport means that you show an authentic interest in others and care about their story, who they are, and their life. That property may have been more significant to him for reasons I wouldn't understand unless I knew his history. For me, it's not about getting what I want. That's not the win. A big part of doing business is connecting with people first, and you do that by being yourself and finding commonality with them. At times, the only thing you will walk away with is that connection, and that's okay.

In an hourlong meeting, we spoke about family, children, and his life, and Cooper didn't seem to hold anything back. We were approaching the end of the meeting when I mentioned, "I forgot, we're here because we want to buy your property. I got caught up in our conversation, it almost slipped my mind."

"What do you want to do with the property?" Cooper questioned.

"We want to put a drugstore on it."

Without hesitating, he stood up, smiled warmly, and jauntily announced, "I'll sell it to you, Chuck!"

Cooper and I were now friends.

"How much?" I asked. When he replied, I said, "Okay, we'll send you a contract." I got up, shook his hand. and said, "It was great meeting you."

When we left his office, Tim turned to me, elated, and said, "I can't believe we got the deal!"

"Yes. It helps to just have a genuine conversation first."

People want to do business with friends.

My best asset in business is being able to communicate with people. It's important for people to get to know you. If you want to be successful in business—or in life, for that matter—remember that when people *like* you, they are more *likely* to do business with you. It doesn't matter who you are; if you're unpretentious and nice to someone, it helps. It's important to make a genuine connection with people on what is important to them. People want to know you see, hear, and genuinely care about them.

———•———

I still have a hard time considering myself wealthy because business is scary. Watch the news. You can lose wealth faster than you'd believe possible. You've seen the news reports on businesses that have closed. Things happen. Uncertainty in the market can cause stocks to fall significantly. There are celebrities and athletes who have squandered their wealth, and people that hit the lottery for millions of dollars and forget about taxes. I know extremely wealthy people who have lost their wealth, which is why it always feels a little borrowed. When I bought my first airplane, I asked myself, *Is this my life? Can I really afford this?* I think questioning yourself keeps you on your game. *If you get cocky and don't question yourself when you are making financial decisions, you face the risk of losing it all.*

I don't take anything for granted. I have a level of nervousness that keeps my edge. Like a fighter pilot, if you don't have adrenaline going, you might lose it. I think that's true with anyone who's good at what they do because it's beneficial during stressful moments.

When people think of success, they think of money. However, money isn't the determination of success; there is a process that brings about the feeling of being successful. It's realizing that what you are building or doing is working, and then constantly raising the bar. It's achieving your goals, feeling fulfilled in having done that, and being happy with the outcome. Although I have been successful in making money, *money isn't success*. If you are the best piano player but you don't play for money, you're still successful. If you're a good parent, it will show in your children.

Success comes in many different ways. While that is my process and definition of success, success means something different to each individual. Don't assign yourself to someone else's definition. *Subscribe to your own definition of success.*

One of the things that has been beneficial to fostering wealth is that I never focused on making money. The goal should be to make something or do something the best you can. If I am going to build a house and sell it just to make money, that's the wrong goal and mentality. I should focus on building the best and most beautiful house that I can—then I'll probably sell it and garner a great return.

When I take on a project, I don't always stick to a firm budget. If my vision changes and I have an idea to make it even better, or I want to try something that will make the development more appealing to a buyer, I need to have financial flexibility. With my experience, I know what's necessary to ensure the value is always there. I don't look at developments to determine how I can make them as economical as possible to maximize profitability. That often backfires, and you don't make money. My concern is always the quality of the developments.

It's hard to tell a struggling person to spend a little more money and convince them that they will do better. Most often the reply is, "Well, I don't have more." True, but that's when you have to step up and find a way to earn more money. Sometimes it's painful, but be creative. There were projects that I wanted to upgrade as I believed they would be more appealing. I scraped together everything I could to do the best job possible. And if you simply don't have it, another way to accomplish that goal is by profit sharing. Find an investor and give them a piece of the deal. Be known for doing quality work that you can take pride in. In time, the financial reward will come.

Good things can take time, and often there are ups and downs that coincide with achieving them. Most people who've made money will tell you that it doesn't happen the first time you try.

————•·•————

Building wealth requires a strong work ethic, but it is also necessary to make sacrifices. Only 1 or 2 percent of the people in the world have acquired the status of being wealthy, and they all gave up something to get there. Not everyone is willing to do that, and you can't expect it. It isn't plausible to expect anyone on my team to work the hours that I do or make the sacrifices to be away from their family to the degree that I am. Keeping the intense schedule that I have isn't easy, but it is necessary to achieve my goals. And, yes, it is a choice. However, I'm quite sure that some of them have things in life that I don't have. Time with family and less stress are as valuable as monetary wealth.

When I made my first million, I didn't say, "Okay, I made a million, I can stop." I bought a bigger house, a more expensive car, and my expenditures increased. People think you stop, but you don't. If becoming a millionaire is the result of a goal, your initial goal doesn't go away, it evolves. You will continue in your pursuit to achieve other goals that are bigger. Sometimes you get aged out, but when you are in business for yourself, there is no finish line.

————•·•————

When I meet people who have seen the projects that we've done, they often ask, "How did you get here?" When I tell them, they reply in disbelief, "So you don't have to have money to go from broke to billions?"

They are surprised when I say, "*I* didn't."

I explain that I've had my power shut off, and I learned how to turn it back on to buy myself a day or two so I could scrounge up the fifty or hundred dollars to pay my bill. If I didn't have it by then, the meter man came out with a heavy padlock. I've had my car repossessed, and now I have a multimillion-dollar car collection. I know what it's like to walk out of my office and realize that my car is no longer in the parking lot. The guy who repossessed my car called, taunting me over the phone, "We've got your car." I had to negotiate with the bank and do all sorts of things to get my car back while I was trying to build a business. At that time, I was in the construction business, and if you didn't pay your workers, there would be consequences. Paying my workers came before paying my car note, and it wasn't an option.

When I look back at all of those things, it wasn't easy. People see where I am now, and they want to be here, but they don't want to go through what I did to get here. I didn't wait and ask for permission to become wealthy—I worked toward being successful, educated myself on personal finance, and hired people to do things that weren't in my area of expertise. But the strategy I maintained is that I never stopped learning from my successes and failures.

Unicorp has done so many outstanding projects in the past that we now receive an abundance of impressive opportunities, but it took years to build this. We've had to work hard to create these opportunities. When you look back, you see that your hard work, reputation, and integrity got you where you are. If someone calls the best brain surgeon in the world, people don't call that person because he or she is lucky. That individual has the reputation and integrity that resulted in the phone call. *Integrity is important in business and in building wealth.*

———•———

People don't realize that relationships take time, and some take years. What's really paying off for us are the relationships we've cultivated. Networking and building strong and ethical relationships over time is an investment. If you continue to do a good job and do what you say, it's like planting orange trees—they keep producing fruit.

The banks I didn't have relationships with prior to the recession became very difficult to work with. When you have a relationship, it makes it harder for someone to look you in the eye and then stab you in the back. When you are growing your business, you have to learn to maintain those relationships. I have nurtured good, solid relationships. If someone does a deal with me, my relationship with him or her is more important than the deal. Even if the deal loses money, they're going to make money. I don't believe in burning friends or anyone. I value relationships.

I had deals go sideways during the recession, and working with those banks was the toughest. My regret is that I didn't realize the importance of having authentic relationships with all my bankers until then. However, that lesson taught me to do that going forward.

———•———

Using partners can certainly speed things up, but you have to prove to your partner that you have a viable business plan. It should be a well-written, thought-out plan; having said that, it's not solely about the plan. People buy into people, and they buy from people with integrity and those they respect. People want to know you aren't going to take advantage of them. If you don't have integrity and aren't respected in business, it can be difficult to get someone to invest with you. There is an old saying: Hang around the people you want to become because you will end up adopting the habits of the people around you. When I did this, I started learning even more. When you are around intelligent, driven people with realistic optimism and integrity, you always do. If your network is comprised of people who aren't driven, focused, or hardworking, or who have other negative habits, you'll spend time emulating them, too. Do business with people who have integrity and principles.

In negotiating the St. Regis deal in Longboat Key, there were many hotel chains who wanted to be on the property. Unicorp negotiated the deal with Marriott, who owns the St. Regis and Ritz-Carlton brands. Once we made that deal, another opportunity arose. Many developers were pursuing the Ritz-Carlton Residences in Orlando, and we were able to land that opportunity as well. How? We leveraged the opportunity for the Ritz-Carlton Residences by leveraging our successful track record and relationship with Marriott.

When you are an entrepreneur, it's easy to work more than you would if you worked for someone else. The business is yours, and no one is going to invest in it exactly the way you would. And you probably won't see a finish line anywhere that indicates you can stop. Work extremely hard and establish your goals, but work *smart*. Ask yourself: Do you own your own business, or does your business own you? An essential aspect of building a truly successful business is that it can run in your absence.

I can tell when I am beginning to take on too much; I start feeling stressed. Then I try to back off a bit. When I reach my capacity, I can scale my organization or back down. I don't want to take away from my quality of life, so I manage it accordingly. I have a family, and I want to have an enjoyable life outside of work. When you're running too hard and pushing yourself, your body will definitely tell you when you need to slow down. Pay attention. *Your health is wealth, too.*

If you aren't taking life seriously by the time you're in your forties, you probably never will.

—CHUCK WHITTALL

Chapter 1

Caring About People

If you're only in it for the money, long term that's never a good thing. In business, you should endeavor to formulate relationships that you are excited about. You should care about the people you collaborate with and the relationships you build. Caring about people has made my team and me more successful. When I have success, I've been blessed to be able to reward others for the great work they do. I want the people who work with me to continue taking pride in their work and enjoy the success that we have *as a team*.

I think you have to be willing to go out there and try different things in life so you can find that place you belong. And when you do, you learn and evolve by trial and error. Some people get a job and they stay there for life. They don't explore their passions and determine what they like. I am grateful that I have explored life, and in some ways, I still am. But I am passionate, and I love that I am fulfilling my destiny. I've met people who haven't done that. Some individuals have come to work with me because it was a job, an opportunity. At some point, they adopted my passion, understood our purpose and vision, and made Unicorp a career. Others have come with their passion intact, ready to help grow and evolve with the company. They learned that if you are going to settle on a career, put everything into it so you can enjoy and benefit from it. They care about the company. Today, our environment is teeming with passionate individuals—and passion is contagious when you are able to establish what the purpose is.

My team puts forth incredible effort to do well. They take it personally when we have success *and* when problems arise. That's our culture at Unicorp. The culture alone is vital to the success of the company. A toxic culture can contribute to one's downfall.

When it comes to building a winning team, I learned how to get it right. When I walk into my office, I feel excited about what we're doing and positive about the goals we establish. You can do that when the culture is supportive, positive, resilient to challenges, and your employees understand your values and ethics and have a clear vision of your goals. When they can't pinpoint the leadership, that's a problem.

Our corporate environment is fun and upbeat. The younger generation brings energy, and energy feeds off energy. Most young people aren't cynical, which is a reason I like hiring them. They have fresh, innovative ideas, and you have to be receptive to them. When you are, the outcome is that they will generate and contribute more. You have to be a good listener, nurture creativity, and care about your people.

Team-building exercises teach everyone the reasons why working together is necessary. We take on everything as a team. Anyone at Unicorp can step out and take a vacation or handle personal matters because we operate as one. We were able to build a good team by having regular corporate events and outings, celebrating birthdays, victories, and all of the things that essentially make you a family.

One of our hiring practices is to primarily hire Type A personalities because they are organized, self-starters, competitive, and ambitious. As they climb the ladder of success, they help move our company along. The more successful they are, the more successful we are. When you are looking at what is best for the company, you want people who have the ambition to get ahead. Unicorp's culture is one that retains individuals who are self-motivated. I like to inspire my team, but I want people who are instinctively driven.

I look at the people I work with as more than employees; they are my friends. Just as they have a daily obligation to me, I have one to them. There are people who are highly proficient in specific things; you should find those people and give them some freedom to use their expertise. Hire people who do not need to be micromanaged. Give them an idea and let them make it bigger. Show them you care about their success by trusting them to use their creativity.

———

Years ago, I realized that people were making Unicorp a career, not just a job. I was pleased to see them doing whatever it took to accomplish goals and excel in their positions. When it comes to my team, I don't count their hours, I look at what they've completed and if they've done all their tasks. I've been witness to seeing everyone in my accounting department put in whatever time it takes to complete their responsibilities. They are instinctively driven, and they care about the overall success of the company. When the recession hit, several of my team members voluntarily gave more than what was required of them. If that doesn't mean I have a winning team, I don't know what could.

Everyone at Unicorp wants to do their job well, and they do. We don't employ individuals that do subpar work. If someone descends to that level, they won't continue working with us. We have got to be the best at what we do and stay on target. If we don't know what we're aiming for, we will never get there. When we encounter a problem, my team and I work together and focus on finding a solution. *We don't quit.*

In regard to the way you meet people, you never know how your lives will intersect or why, but they will. You may not know the purpose behind each encounter, but time will reveal it. And these meetings are not by coincidence. If you truly care about people, when it is time to do the right thing, you will. When you see someone needs guidance, offer it freely.

On January 12, 2010, a magnitude-7.0 catastrophic earthquake struck Haiti just before four in the afternoon, with the epicenter near the town of Léogâne. I was in my office at Unicorp when I received a call from my church. They told me that some of the local kids, who had gone to Haiti on a mission, were stranded there. The gentleman on the phone expressed, in a serious tone, "We've got to get down to Haiti. We have connections for some off-duty Navy SEALs and Army Rangers, and we want to get the kids out, but we need a way to get them down there."

One of the kids was Taylor, a seventeen-year-old girl who attended the same school as my daughter, Riley, although they didn't know one another.

I said, "Use my plane. It's ready to go."

He accepted, and I made the arrangements for them.

My plane was going to take off shortly after four o'clock that next afternoon, but my pilot called and informed me, "Chuck, there's no one here with an overflight permit. We can't go without you." They couldn't fly over Cuba and the Dominican Republic without me on the plane. I was at my office when I called my wife, Ronna, and asked, "Can you pack some clothes for me? I'm going to Haiti."

"What?" she exclaimed, because she'd heard the news of the earthquake.

"Please, get my passport for me, Ronna. I've got to go."

I drove home, grabbed my things, and went straight to the airport. The news was saturated with the massive devastation, and it was getting worse with each report. I boarded my plane with two Navy SEALs, two Army Rangers, and two other gentlemen. After landing in the Dominican Republic, we went to the hotel and checked in. Shortly thereafter, I went to dinner with the guys and helped devise an extraction plan to get the kids home safely. We agreed to convene in the lobby at 4:00 a.m. and head to Haiti.

When I tried to leave my hotel room at 3:45 a.m., I realized my door handle was broken. I couldn't get out of my room. I had to call hotel security and have them come and let me out. We went to the airport and paid cash to hire four helicopter pilots to take us to Haiti to rescue the kids. At home, a friend of mine, Bud Bennington, was working with the government to line up a Black Hawk helicopter to get the kids as well.

Taylor told me while they were waiting on the ground, "The whole time we saw helicopters, we would run and wave, but it wasn't our turn to go. Finally, one helicopter landed, and these armed mercenaries jumped out of it strapped with guns. They sat us down and stated, 'This has to happen quickly; it's going to be very fast. Just listen to what we say. Just leave everything.' They grabbed us one at a time, threw us onto the helicopters and got us up in the air. Everything looked like splinters before we reached any height. They took us to the Dominican Republic, and after nine hours at the military base, we boarded a large plane home."

A gentleman who'd won the lottery chartered the Tampa Bay Buccaneers' plane and flew it to the Dominican Republic, where he waited for the kids to safely board the plane. I flew home by myself because the mercenaries stayed behind to continue in their rescue efforts.

Along with Taylor and the other kids, the plane was filled with as many people as it could hold. I arrived in time to watch a brave young girl, bruised and resilient, rush to make her way over to her parents and twin brother, Travis. I can't possibly put into words the emotional reunion when her parents held their daughter in their arms. Tearful yet heartened, Taylor's mother gently turned her toward me and said, "Tay, this is one of the men who helped rescue you, Chuck Whittall."

Taylor gave me a heartfelt, impromptu hug as she thanked me. I could sense her relief and only imagine what she and the other kids had experienced—and what those in Haiti were suffering through. That catastrophic earthquake, according to the Haitian government, claimed the lives of approximately 316,000 people and injured a reported 300,000. I was grateful that the collective efforts of everyone involved brought the children home safely.

Through the years, Taylor has stayed in touch with me. She gifted me with a book she had written, sharing the details of her experience in Haiti, as well as her rescue. Prior to the tragedy, Taylor hadn't known Riley, and I hadn't known her parents. Five years later, in her last semester of college, I hired Taylor as my personal assistant and to handle social media at Unicorp. Taylor is now an important part of our Unicorp family.

Being successful should mean that you acknowledge your blessings and don't take them for granted. When you have the opportunity to use your blessings to help others, be generous and don't hesitate. You never know who you will be reaching for and how that experience will affect you. *I am forever changed.*

———

I had just stepped out onto the sidewalk on a wintery night in downtown Chicago in 2013. I was leaving a business dinner and heading back to my hotel. I was waiting next to the valet as my cab pulled up. A woman came out of the restaurant and stood beside me. I opened the door, turned to her, and asked, "Are you waiting for a cab?"

"I am," she replied. "But I can get the next one."

I stepped aside, presenting the empty back seat, "You're more than welcome to share this cab," I offered as I glanced at the heavy snowfall claiming the sky and blanketing the streets and tops of cars.

"Thank you, I appreciate that," she said, and climbed inside the cab.

"Where are you going?" I asked as I got in and shut the door.

"Trump Tower."

"Are you staying there?"

She said, "Yes, I am."

"Oh, what does your husband do?" I asked, making conversation, but I didn't mean to sound dismissive of her. Yet it may have seemed that way.

She didn't say; instead she replied candidly, "You can look me up. I'm Jan Fields," she stated and then shook my hand.

I apologized for the assumption and asked her to tell me her story. While the driver took great care on the snow-covered streets, Jan began talking about her remarkable career and how she started working at the front counter of a McDonald's in Dayton, Ohio, in 1978 for $2.65 per hour cooking french fries. Over the years, Jan explained how her hard work, dedication, and being an advocate for people development elevated her from the bottom level of McDonald's to the executive suite. Jan was appointed executive vice president and then chief operating officer of McDonald's USA. In 2010, Jan became the president of McDonald's USA, overseeing fourteen thousand restaurants across the United States. She never completed college. Her impressive career with McDonald's spanned thirty-four years. Jan Fields worked her way up from the ground floor to become a multimillionaire, and in 2012 she was recognized as number 25 on *Fortune*'s list of "50 Most Powerful Women in Business" and was also listed among *Forbes*'s "The World's 100 Most Powerful Women." You never know whom you may be sharing a cab ride with, so be humble.

Success isn't for one gender, one race, or one person. It's for those who believe they can be successful and are willing to pay the price, make the sacrifices, work hard, have integrity, and persevere. Success isn't free; *there is a hefty price to pay.*

There isn't one way to achieve success void of challenges to become a millionaire or billionaire, and the opportunity to be successful exists for anyone who is hungry enough to work for it. People quit because it's too challenging or it's taking too long. At times, people are on the cusp of success, but they quit before they achieve it. Why is that? They failed to see their vision all the way through.

Although it was my path, success is not *solely* achieved by starting your own company—being an entrepreneur. You can be part of a company and live the American Dream, but a commonality for many successful individuals is that we truly care about the people we serve and the job that we do.

When it comes to people, care to know their story. Ask about their life and listen because you will always learn something or be inspired by what they have accomplished or overcome.

Building a billion-dollar company takes a great deal of time. There is intrigue in making a lot of money, and it is exciting. However, when you seek those rewards, you are bound to sacrifice something. You have to reflect on your life as you go through it and find balance.

—CHUCK WHITTALL

Chapter 8

The Deal that Led to Billions

I began this journey when I was a kid. I didn't know it at the time; I couldn't have. But I was drawn to uncover what life offered and what I needed to do to claim it. I can't say that my journey has been without adversity, because I've faced it, but even with the barriers and adversity I've encountered, I've had success when I pushed through. If you don't, you will never know how great you could have been, what you may have accomplished, and if that deal was worth billions. Sometimes the best deal you will ever make will come when you've learned from life.

People often ask how I became successful and what I did differently than others. What was the deal that made Unicorp a billion-dollar company? *The deal that led to billions was one that I made with myself.* It was to:

1. Focus on being the best and outdo your competition
2. Sustain optimism

3. Become extremely knowledgeable in your industry
4. Be confident in your decisions
5. Have a concise, innovative vision
6. Sustain an unquestionable work ethic
7. Become a good listener
8. Remain disciplined
9. Operate with integrity
10. Build a strong infrastructure
11. Communicate effectively
12. Network with like-minded individuals
13. Delegate and trust the experts
14. Possess great time-management skills
15. Remain passionate
16. Know your purpose
17. Make time to recharge
18. Have faith
19. Pay attention to the details
20. Have the perseverance to move forward
21. Have fun, love life, and celebrate the victories

Consistently doing these things is how I went from being a kid with the dream of one day being successful enough to buy any pair of shoes I wanted, to being the owner of a successful, billion-dollar real estate development company who buys more shoes than I probably need. *There is no big deal that makes someone a billionaire; it's a slow climb of the ladder.*

When you do the things listed above habitually, your positive reputation will precede you, and people will want to do business with you. Those habits will generate more opportunities, which is how Unicorp evolved into a billion-dollar company.

When you are confident and good at what you do, people will be interested in working with you. But when you are *great* at what you do, people will find you the same way they go out of their way to seek out the best cardiothoracic surgeons, neurosurgeons, financial advisors, attorneys, athletes, musicians, architects, and so forth.

Fortunes are made and lost in real estate, and at some point you will lose. I don't mind taking the risk, because I am confident and optimistic when I enter into a transaction. If I weren't confident, I wouldn't do it. The deals I enter into have multiple agreements and layers, and it is imperative to know how to manage risk. I can generally foresee an outcome because I pay close attention to the details when I make an assessment of an opportunity. However, there is always some degree of uncertainty with any development project.

There are exceptions to most things, and although acquiring wealth can happen instantly, for most, building wealth takes time. A friend of mine declared, "Just because you have a baseball bat in your hand doesn't mean you are ready to play in the major leagues. You're not. You have to earn it, work for it, strive for it." It takes time and a special set of skills.

If you build an aesthetically pleasing place, people will want to go there to eat, visit, or live. I have no doubt that people will go to the places we develop because they are appealing to the senses. Architectural elements and landscape are a critical combination when you keep your target audience in mind. I utilize landscaping because it creates warm, inviting, and healthier environments that people select as a preferred place to be. Many people gravitate toward water, art, and colorful flowers. Water and landscape are natural to the environment, and art is within humans. When you combine all three, it makes our developments personal, and we want people to have a personal experience. In particular, I love landscapes that feel as though they are organic to the environment, while complementing the theme or structure we've built.

When you go to a place that you like, you may not know the reason, but your mind and your eyes pick up on what made it a nice place. Even if you can't discern precisely what it is, you notice that someone paid attention to the details and appreciated how everything came together. We pay close attention to the details because we know you do.

During my travels, I've explored Europe's best destinations. One place I was fascinated by was Positano, Italy. They have the ocean, beautiful flowers, and incredible architecture. I marvel at the integrity and distinctiveness of the designs and the way people are so engaged when they observe them. I study all types of designs and gain as much knowledge as I can, and I try to incorporate those types of features into my developments. Why? Tourists travel there for a reason. These are places that have stood the test of time.

When we build hotels, we don't wing it. I invest time in traveling around the world, visiting dozens of five-star hotels to see what they've done and what makes them successful. I study their entire operation. I am educating myself so I, too, can operate like other successful hotels. If I wanted to have a prosperous coffee shop, I would do the same thing. Learning takes research, time, and patience. You have to learn before you begin, and you must be willing to be a good student. Observe what people are doing and it can help you grow. Studying other properties doesn't mean you should copy them, but it may help you take an idea to the next level or spawn creativity in a way you have yet to imagine, further enhancing your own vision. Naturally, you will make mistakes—but don't get caught up in them or become discouraged. Continue on.

My first development deal was a flip. I sold it to a timeshare mogul and made $25,000. I put another property under contract for $1 million, but Lee and I couldn't afford to close on it. The opportunity was too good to lose, so we found a way to proceed. We negotiated time on the contract and sold it to Hops Restaurant Bar & Brewery for $1.3 million. When we went to close, we had the seller in one room, the buyer in another, and we were in a third room. The seller and buyer had no idea that we were in the middle of the transaction simultaneously selling and buying. We made $300,000 on that deal, and it was the first time Lee and I made a profit that was substantial. If you want something, figure out how to get it. To celebrate, we both went out and bought ourselves a gold Rolex.

At the same time, Lee and I secured the deal with three drugstores and made a couple of million dollars each. From then on, drugstores became our focus. We averaged a million to a million and a half per store. It wasn't until that point, when we had more business flowing in, that we understood our value. No deal was too small, but when we reached another level where business was coming to us, that's when we set a floor. If we couldn't make a million dollars, we wouldn't take the project. But if we did ten $1 million deals, we made $10 million. We looked at those transactions as bread-and-butter deals. They weren't too small, and they were less risky. When you do a $100 million deal, there is more risk and capital involved.

Unicorp is a preferred developer for the Wawa convenience store chain, and we do a lot of them. They are safe-credit tenant deals, and we don't have any issues with the tenant paying. Deals like that don't take you to the edge. You make less money, but you have significantly less risk.

As I became more experienced and confident in my abilities, I increased the size of the deals. I was taking larger risks, and larger risks bring larger returns. Again, what contributed to making us extremely successful is that we didn't have financial partners.

The pivotal point came when I bought out my partner. Although the timing spilled into a recession, it was a great move going forward. What made the turn for Unicorp was selling $263 million in assets to Excel Trust. It capitalized us. We took those funds and reinvested them. *You cannot hold your capital too tightly.* If we make $20 million on a deal, we invest it into two deals, and those two deals become four deals and so on. That's how you grow exponentially. I don't make money just to sit on it. We work to find the best deals and pounce on them. If it requires more capital, we put it in. Our goal is to make wise investments. Real estate development is a multifaceted business; when you become educated and confident, don't be afraid to *think big.*

Although I have access to troves of market research, which is beneficial, and making great investments is a gut decision, there is still more to it. It's being an expert at what we do. I learned the real estate business, and I am fascinated by taking a raw piece of land and creating a place that becomes a part of people's lives, where they work, dine, shop, or live.

I am constantly studying the market and following the trends so I can rely on what I know. Complex decision-making is necessary, and you have to trust the experts. That's what they are there for. If there is a catastrophic event, like a failure in the economy, obviously we can't control that. There are occasions when things don't turn out the way we expect, but most of the time they do. People ask if we lose money. Generally, no, because we know what we're doing. We don't operate on ego; we shy away from doing projects that are not in our area of expertise.

In real estate development, education is critical in relation to decision-making. Before I begin a project, I work out a complete business plan. In my business plan, I outline the project from inception to completion. I need to understand what we are doing before we turn the first shovel of dirt. If you want to be in real estate development, determine what your plan or vision is and start there.

SpaceX is growing, NASA is surging, and Cape Canaveral is the site of a lot of new space-related initiatives. I was informed of their growth and asked to look at a great piece of property by Kennedy Space Center in Cape Canaveral. I agreed and went with two of my team members to the specified location. When I saw it, my gut told me that the property wasn't in the right area. Even though there is a lot of growth at Kennedy Space Center, I didn't get the sense that people were living in the immediate area. There were nice communities situated merely a half-hour away. After seeing them, I concluded that the engineers would rather live in more affluent areas and make the thirty-minute commute than have Unicorp come in and develop that particular area. It came down to location.

If I worked at NASA and made the salary of an engineer, the question would be, Where do I want to live? If I were willing to make that commute, others may feel the same way. Therefore, I wasn't willing to take the risk.

In any development or project I do, I always try to put myself in the place of the consumer. Would I eat here? Would I go here? Would I work here? Choices are based on desire. Real estate has to be in places that people want to be, which is the reason I would only build something where I would want to work, eat, or live. When you pick B locations that are not where people want to go, you are not gaining the focus of the masses, and it's critical to do so—success depends on it. If you select a good neighborhood that is highly sought-after, when you go to sell your house, it's going to be easier. If you choose a neighborhood that's not as desirable, doesn't have great schools or quality shopping, it's harder to sell your house. The same goes for commercial retail developments. If you put things in a place where people want to be, you will do well. And as stated, that comes down to location. *Location is the most important aspect of the real estate business.*

During the great recession, we learned that B locations turn into C locations. If they are somewhat desirable, they become undesirable in a bad market. We will only do A deals in A+ locations.

Pride can get the best of you if you let it, so don't. You have to know when to cut your losses. I bought a piece of property, and even though we theorized it was a B+ property at best, I thought it was a stronger market. It just wasn't doing what we expected it to do. I decided to put the property up for sale and move past it. On that occasion, I'd gone against my own advice of picking A+ locations. In hindsight, I could definitely tell the difference. It was difficult to make that real estate location go positively. As opposed to fighting what was inevitable, we sold it for a small financial loss. It reaffirmed that A locations are the only thing we can do.

You have to choose the right location, and most often I look for my own properties. I started out that way. Ronna and I would get in the car, drive around, and look at houses in appealing neighborhoods. We would imagine that one day we would have a beautiful home in a picturesque neighborhood, too. If you pay attention to the community as a whole, you can see when houses are selling and when shopping centers are full or half empty. That's how I educated myself. When I got into commercial real estate, I did the same thing. I'd drive around and say, "That's a great piece of property," and I'd use my imagination and envision what I'd put on that site. People often approach me about specific locations, and I can quickly discern if I like them or not. If I believe it's going to work, then I'll buy it. If it's not a hard yes, it's a no. If I *think* I can make it work—that's a no. I have to know it's going to work. I rely on my gut more than market studies, but I am not infallible. I make mistakes. However, there are only a few projects I've completed that haven't made what I expected. I work hard to make good decisions.

The biggest losses I see in real estate development transpire when people buy the wrong property and build the wrong product on it. Choosing the wrong location and executing on it is one of the worst things you can do. For instance, would you open a sandwich shop in a thriving city such as New York, where you have millions of square feet of office space around it? Or would you open it in a neighborhood where people are at work the majority of the day?

Be cognizant of people who try to talk you into buying a property. Be cautious and take time to do your own due diligence on any property. People have tried to convince me that something was good, but that is an assessment *I* need to make. Good things sell themselves. Again, you need to do your own research and determine whether something is worth the investment. Don't buy it just because someone told you that it's good. *You don't know their motivation.*

You have to be a forward-thinker and keep up with the trends of society. I've watched some of the giants of the world, like Sears,

Kmart, J. C. Penney, and Lord & Taylor, who didn't evolve their business with the marketplace. They failed and became obsolete. That's one of the reasons why Walmart is doing next-day delivery—they evolved to keep up with competitors. If you think you should continue doing something the same way because it has always been the process, then you will remain stagnant. Before you know it, the current generation will show you how wrong you are. To be prosperous and profitable, *be the trendsetter.* You can follow the market and adapt to the market you are following, but you can set the trends, too. Our goal is to be innovative.

The best properties that have the best rate of return for Unicorp are urban redevelopments. Those are properties that were built for one purpose but weren't built to their highest and best use in today's market. We demolish those properties and rebuild them with more density. We did that with a property in Michigan. There was an office building standing on fourteen valuable acres. When I analyzed the property to create a vision for it, innovation caused me to question why there were thirteen acres of parking. I envisioned building a parking garage and using the remaining twelve acres for additional buildings. When the property went up for sale, the other developers didn't have the vision I did. I discovered that what they saw was an office building that had to be remodeled, which would increase its value a little bit more. From my perspective, the parking lot needed to be remodeled and replaced with buildings. I bought the property, and that's just what we did. It has been highly profitable for us, as Unicorp will exceed a $100 million profit on that deal. Redevelopment and turning things into their highest and best use is where we get the largest rate of return. *It comes down to vision. It's imperative to look at things through a different lens.*

As I've stated, some properties find me; however, when we invest in commercial real estate, I generally find the best properties in coastal areas. Florida, New York, Texas, California, North Carolina, and Washington, DC, are some of the primary areas in the country where Unicorp develops. Understand your business and the politics that go along with it. Understand that the public sector is involved as a stakeholder. This is why it's important to give the public something they will find value in.

People want to make money, and they want to make it fast. They are quick to go after big deals before they understand all of the intricacies of real estate development. Every time we develop a property, we learn something of value. I recall one of my early lessons was that you don't get the big deal without doing the little deals.

My first big transaction was Baldwin Park for $100 million, and we did that well because we had completed several little deals before then. Eventually, I sold off those little deals. But I discovered that with big deals come big problems. When you get into big deals, you have to be able to backstop them—be able to write the check. Contractors find problems all the time, and when that happens, they will charge you for them. Typically, they are issues that you would be less inclined to expect. Even with the best plan, it's not plausible to adequately prepare for every fraction of adversity that will happen in the process, and that can be costly. Be apprised that there are constant reconfigurations. The contractor may hit you with change orders, and you will have to pay them. In real estate development, unforeseen conditions materialize all the time, and it's typically something subsurface that you didn't anticipate. The contractor may run the power differently than what was expected, and it becomes more expensive. In business, be prepared for situations that are not predictable, and that's the same with life. I have a non-defeatist attitude. *If something comes my way, I am going to deal with it. That is the best way to persevere.*

You can be profitable if you take the time to learn the real estate development business and don't rush to grow too quickly. Although there are always exceptions, in general, it takes time to amass a large amount of wealth. It took me forty years to get here, and I'm not done. I want to keep working.

My position in life has always been to never give up. Don't stop until you're dead. I can't make every deal, but I have a competitive nature and I am most competitive with myself. The bottom line is that before you let something go—give it your all.

I often get calls where people have a property they think I might be interested in. I listen and discuss the opportunity because you never know what may come of it. Sometimes the property isn't what we're looking for, and that's okay, because I meet incredible people in the process.

One particular day, I was in my office and had just finished a call on a development we were doing in Michigan. Another call came in from a guy with a solid reputation.

He said, "Hey, Chuck. I have this deal available. I already bought the property. It's three million. What would you pay me?"

I was already knowledgeable about the property. Yet I asked additional questions and listened to the specifics and determined that I did want the property.

I told him, "Okay, I'll give you three million, with a thirty-day inspection period and a sixty-day closing."

He replied, "I'll get back to you."

The next day, I heard from his CFO that they had received another offer, for $3.1 million, with a thirty-day inspection period and a thirty-day closing. It was a better offer, so they were going with it. I was upset, and I couldn't sleep because I had lost the deal. I know I can't have everything, but upon reflection, I hadn't done everything to keep it. The following morning, I woke up at 5:00 a.m. and sent him an email stating, "You represent a public company and are obligated to do what's best for your stockholders. I'm going to offer you $3.3 million with no inspection period and I'll give you $100,000 in cash today. We'll close in thirty days." I was pleased when he replied early that same morning and agreed. Unicorp now owns the property.

By now, you know that I am in real estate development because I enjoy it, not because I have to do it. If I'm going to be involved with something, I make a conscious decision to do so. Why did I get this deal? Sure, I wasn't willing to accept that someone else beat me, but it goes beyond competitiveness. It was that I want to be the best version of myself I can be. If someone legitimately beats me, I can accept that, but I have to give it my all—in everything I do. You won't get everything, but don't give up until you've given it every single thing you have. Look at the details, work the numbers, and if it makes sense—fight for it. When you have the capital, you have the choice.

The act of practicing and sustaining an optimistic mindset can shift your outlook. It's a coping mechanism when challenges or difficult life situations arise. I am an optimistic person, and that keeps me happy. I look at the good side of everything, although I am acutely conscious of what's on the other side. I don't have to go somewhere or do something to put me in a happy state. And it's not possible for someone to remove my optimistic mindset either.

One negative person can bring down an entire staff and infect your business culture, home environment—practically anywhere.

You want people focused on how good things are rather than how negative they are. Work to create positive environments by changing the topic and pointing out the favorable attributes of a situation. Encourage and be open to creative solutions or leave the conversation—but avoid negativity any way you can. Pay attention to the optics because they matter.

There are people who just don't want to be happy. Some have a chip on their shoulder because something happened in their life they won't let go of. They feel that they are owed something, which isn't a healthy perspective. You can't necessarily change, control, or fix them, but you can move on.

There are men and women in the military who've sacrificed for this country and met dire, unimaginable consequences despite their bravery, and still, they fight to persevere. They don't know how to quit. Some people have one bad thing happen in life and they give up. They never considered perseverance as an option. I see people who refuse to try. The gift that some people have causes them to know they need to accomplish something, and that comes from within.

Michael Jordan was built to be a great athlete; I was not. I was hardwired to have optimism. I know people who hold on to bad things that have happened in their lives. If that's what is weighing you down or dragging you backward, you aren't going to move forward. People need to make the choice to let things go. If you aren't moving forward, the question becomes, Why not? That was the past.

I'm not angry about the things that happened in my life, as they are what shaped me. The way I see it is, the good things have eclipsed the bad. Only you can choose to have a better life for yourself. When I go out and speak, I often ask, "How many of you are going to have a good life?" The individuals who raise their hands are going to have the opportunity to do so. Make the choice to say, "To hell with all that—this is what I'm going to do. I am blessed because I've made the choice that nothing will hold me back." Your degree of success will depend on your mindset, what you believe.

During the period when I went to court with the guy who was trying to steal our house, I was down, and I'm not used to being down. I didn't have anyone tell me to get my ass up. I had to figure it out and change my situation. I saw the Anthony Robbins *Personal Power* tape advertised on television and bought it. I was honest enough to say, *I need a kick in the ass—a push.* It helped me get motivated, and from there I refused to relinquish my faith, optimism, confidence in my abilities, or anything else that would keep me from my destiny.

During the times I've encountered barriers that seemed impassable or nearly crippling, I never had anyone tell me to get up and keep going. I had to determine if I still wanted to accomplish what I set out to do—and do it. If you're fortunate enough to have someone encourage you to keep going, accept the challenge and regain your strength to fight through whatever obstacles you're facing. It's the only way to persevere! There are people who like to see you fall—but you have to get back up.

There are habits that I don't deviate from, and they have helped me become successful in business and my personal life:

1. *Be optimistic.*
2. *Always plan your day.*
3. *Dress for success.* People notice what you wear, how you look, and the way you carry yourself. I have my own sense of style. I used to wear suits all the time; now I wear blue jeans and a jacket.

4. *Remember that your words matter.* People pay attention to the details, right down to what you say—so do what you say.

5. *Always be respectful and nice to people.* I have a friend who is an architect. He is successful in his career, a great guy, and people genuinely like him. Why? Because he maintains that "being nice is free." Who would you want to do business with, someone you like or don't like? If you aren't likeable, people may not want to do business with you.

6. *Be involved in every aspect of your business.* When you are involved, people strive to be better because they know you care. Don't think you are any better than anyone else in your company. If you see something that needs to be done, do it. If weeds need to be picked, be willing to pick the weeds.

7. *Be financially generous.* Some people try to hold on to every dollar they make. I find that it is important to be generous to your employees. You don't want to hire incredible talent and then lose them because you aren't willing to pay them properly. To compete at a high level, you need a high-level team.

8. *Don't try to be the smartest person in the room.* When you hire experts for their knowledge, be willing to accept what they say and learn from them.

9. *Pay attention to the details.* They matter, and people notice.

10. *Don't let your business run you; you run your business.*

You can go through tough times, but fight to get to the other side. When you come out of adversity, you will appreciate what you were able to accomplish because life will be better than you've ever imagined.

—CHUCK WHITTALL

Chapter 9

Sustaining Wealth

I was having a discussion with a friend about the escalating number of people who are getting into debt nowadays, and its associated problems. It's not possible for everyone to live without debt. People have to put money down to buy a house or a car, they have medical bills, college tuition, and things like that, but slowly, over time, you want to avoid buying or doing things you can't afford. You don't want to get into credit card debt because the interest rates are absolutely insane. And if that happens, the outcome is that you will end up paying so much money in interest that it becomes difficult to get ahead. Buy things slowly. Pay things off when you have the ability to do so. Make extra payments on your house when you can.

In the beginning, I went into debt. But I quickly realized that to be successful, I had to get out of debt and become creditworthy, which I did. I knew I wanted to be debt free on our house, so we bought fixer-uppers, lived in them, and put each one up for sale. During that time, Ronna and I lived in eleven houses over ten years. I was able to pay off our house after a number of years, and I never got into residential debt again.

Initially, when I started my development company, I didn't need partners because I had taken money that I'd earned and invested it myself. That money came from saving, and I was able to save because I avoided going into debt.

For instance, start with your car. Don't be anxious to buy a new one. Buy what you can afford and get it paid off. Then when you are ready to buy a new one, trade in the old one, add some cash, and stay out of debt. It is disheartening when I hear of or see people drowning in payments. The number-one thing that causes divorce in America is financial struggles; many people get divorced because they fight over money. And if you get divorced, you'll likely lose half your money, and then you may end up further in debt.

I believe I moved forward much quicker in my career by not getting saddled with debt. I was willing to work two or three jobs if necessary to remain financially responsible. When you are in debt, you lose freedom, because you have to work for someone, which makes it hard to be in business for yourself. Extensive debt will keep you working all the time, and that alone can change your quality of life—and affect your health. I learned to make decisions that gave me the financial freedom to invest money and do different things. *The primary starting point is to be frugal and save.* I did this when I ate bologna sandwiches until I was able to accomplish financial goals and furnish my apartment.

If you have to work two jobs to pay off your debt, or debt from college—do it. Don't let your ego talk you out of it. When you start making money, bank it instead of buying more things. Once you have money in the bank, *you* can become an investor. Start small, complete that project, and go from one investment to another and other. Eventually, you will have the potential to earn a lot of money.

As you continue to mature in your career, your house and toys will grow with you. If you grow them at a level where you can afford to pay for them, you will grow quicker and stronger. Don't live beyond your means.

The advice that was given to me about debt came when I turned nineteen years old. I was making okay money, but not a large amount. I went out and bought a sports car, a boat, a truck, and was spending money like a drunken sailor. Although the optics made it appear that I was getting ahead, I wasn't. I found myself working all the time to pay for my *things*.

After hearing a church service on how debt strangles you, I decided to get out of debt. I sold my house and took the equity to pay cash for a cheaper house and have never had a mortgage since. My homes have gotten bigger, but I have stayed out of debt. Then I gained the financial freedom to take the money I was earning and invest it into building a business, which was significantly wiser than buying the next toy. As a result, I made enough money so that I can buy the toys I want. The advice is that if you try to buy the toys and the big house in the beginning, you will have a big house and toys that you will be struggling to make the payments on. It will end right there, and you won't get further ahead. In order to sustain wealth, you have to build it.

It can take a lifetime to become wealthy, but if you observe *Forbes*'s list of the world's richest people, it changes over time. Why? Sometimes it's just difficult staying in one position. And when wealth is passed along, at times heirs can lose part of the fortune.

Sustaining wealth isn't solely about money. That's just part of it. Yes, it's about making solid financial decisions and investments, and managing your money, but wealth is whatever possessions you have that are valuable to you. It can be human capital—your health, education, spirituality, and the contributions you make for others.

———•———

Investing in commercial real estate is unbelievably capital intensive—even with the smallest of deals. It's wise to begin with small deals and learn from them while taking on less risk.

How do you start off in the beginning? As mentioned, I was a home flipper. I bought homes, fixed them up, and sold them. In the beginning, I made $10,000, then $20,000, and before I knew it, I had $40,000 or $50,000 in the bank. Most banks require you to put down 30 percent or so on commercial deals, so you must save and be prepared. When you get $50,000 in the bank, take it and invest in a small, $150,000 development. Put down $40,000 and make something of it. Then sell the property for $210,000 or more. Do it again—and wealth builds. People think it happens quickly, but I've been in the business for over two decades to get to this point in my life. With *patience* and *persistence*, it is possible for almost anyone to become wealthy over time.

I mentioned that you should start out by investing in small deals to remove the negative connotation that you can't make money on them. I started out with small deals, reinvested, and those little deals gave me the investment capital to do bigger and bigger deals. The strategy that worked was to increase the size of my deals. You have to be willing to make $5,000 before you make $10,000. It took years to get to where I am, and I'm not the biggest fish in the pond, but I'm swimming with them.

After Ronna and I were married, one of our small businesses was a vending business. We purchased roughly twenty vending machines and determined what our niche would be. We filled the vending machines with items that were needed in a restroom, stuck them in the back of my car, and drove to various restaurants where they agreed to place them. We would go back to the restaurants, collect the quarters, restock the machines, and then use those profits to buy more machines. Those are the small things that help you make money. Don't be afraid to be creative or do the work. Sometimes you make money a quarter at a time, but it adds up.

Some of my tenants have rented space from me to start their own business. One of them got a loan and opened a sub shop. Their first location was successful, and so they opened a second. Before I knew it, they had six or eight sub shops, and they were doing well with them. I've seen several of our tenants do that over the years. Industrious people who want to build a business don't just make the investment—they rely on their work ethic and passion, too.

------◆------

I learned to respect money from a young age and went from being broke to having a billion-dollar company. There were numerous lessons in between that led me to understand how to sustain wealth. There can be costly mistakes in real estate; some are unavoidable. However, in business in general, there are financial strategies to keep you from going into debt and sustain your wealth or what you have. Each time I made a poor decision, rather than feel sorry for myself, I learned what I should have done. Below I've identified eight necessary habits for sustaining wealth:

1. *Set goals.* If you haven't established a goal, you will never know when you have reached it. Once wealth is accumulated, you must continue to build on it. So determine where you want your capital to be in a year, and in the next decade, as well. Lay out a safe road map to achieve your desired goal and be realistic. Do not take an aggressive approach, but lean more toward the conservative side once you have generated wealth. Be aggressive in your early career, but transition to being more conservative as you get older.

2. *Build up enough to have a nest egg.* At the beginning of your career, you may have to go into debt to some extent because you have nothing. I position myself so that I can afford to walk away from every individual investment I make. I invest in many things, with the understanding that they all may not pay off.

3. *Be cautious of stockbrokers seeking to invest your money.* Stockbrokers are fee-driven, and they make their money regardless of whether or not you make money. Take time to become knowledgeable about finances. Once you make money, there are plenty of people who are going to pitch you on why you should put your money with them instead of somewhere else. Have good attorneys, accountants, and financial advisors. If someone wants you to invest, make sure everyone signs off on it. The same goes for charities. They will come your way, but you need to vet them. Unicorp has a board, and I run everything through my CFO and in-house legal counsel. I don't make quick decisions on the phone. We want to understand who the charitable recipients are. Be cautious.

4. *When you are younger, you make money. When you are older, you manage it.* Where you keep your cash and why you keep it there matters. Keep your money with firms that offer you more than you offer them. I want to keep my cash with people I trust will not invest it unwisely. Your financial advisors should work to preserve your capital and protect your assets. Don't forget that you are the one who made the money, and it's your job to oversee and manage it.

5. *Don't rest on your laurels.* Most people I know who have made money say this. The fear of becoming unsuccessful keeps successful people going. People tell me, "Chuck, you don't have to keep working. You can be comfortable the rest of your life." But I don't know that. I don't think there is a finish line. If you've made wealth, it doesn't mean you are done. You still have to manage and sustain it for the next generation. You have to come up with wealth preservation through trusts. I've done it, and not only for the benefit of my daughter, Riley, but for Ronna and me. If something ever became catastrophic— unforeseen events always happen in life—you need to be prepared by having a wealth preservation plan. It took a lot of time with attorneys, accountants, and investment advisors to construct my will and trust. Even without a catastrophic event, it is well worth the time. These tools not only provide you with protection, they have the ability to save millions in taxes, as well.

The bottom line is that I want to ensure I have preserved my wealth. It took a lot of time and hard work to make what I am protecting. You need to have a very large umbrella and insurance policies. Insurance companies offer a barrier between you and those who may want to attack your finances. The wealthier you become, the more you become a target. Any venture we do, we set up a limited liability company (LLC). If something were to happen, it would be isolated within that company. Each LLC does a single piece of business. If something happens, whether or not it is your fault, you need to insulate yourself from other companies you own. A successful restaurateur may have ten restaurants. If he is clever, even if they have the same name, they will all be separate LLCs. In the event an incident occurs, someone can only go after the company where the incident occurred and not the entire chain. This is how you *limit liability*.

6. *A big part of wealth preservation is about knowing when to say no.* My friend John Morgan taught me that. If it's not a hard yes, it's a no. Sure, it can be hard to say no, but it's okay. You don't want to seem like an unsympathetic voice; however, when people come to you for money, it's because they don't have it and there *is* a reason for that. If they are young and they've lost money, there may be a good reason, but be cautious. John told me to invest in the jockey and not the horse. Know who the people are that are coming to you. Make sure they have the track history. When you've made money, there are plenty of people who will want to see your money go to work for them. You have to be discerning. If someone comes to me with an investment, I invest in the jockey, just as people have invested in me. One of my primary lenders is Goldman Sachs. They recognize that I am an expert in real estate development. Goldman Sachs invested in me

because they have faith in what I am doing and my track history. Once you establish that history, people will invest in you. It's important to establish good character and integrity, as they will follow you throughout your life.

7. *You can't be afraid to invest.* You have to believe in yourself. Intelligent people figure a way around things. When you have great financial advisors, legal counsel, or a wealth management team, bounce things off them. Don't be careless. Once you make money, you can't be careless with it.

You can't forget how you made your money and must continue to reinvest. As I get older, I still invest, but a little more cautiously. I don't want to take risks that will outlive my time. I am not going to forget what created my wealth—real estate development. I don't invest in a lot of stocks; I invest in what I know and do what I do best.

What has helped in the growth of our company is truly being an investment firm. There are many merchant builders who develop, build, and sell. Then there are those who hold real estate and develop cash flow. We have done both. We build and sell and collect cash. Despite slower or precarious times, we have cash flow to fall back on, and banks want to see that. I don't want to have a wad of cash and in the next few months have nothing because I invested it all. You must maintain a reasonable percentage of pure cash along with your investments, which is generally 10 to 20 percent of your net worth. Holding income-producing assets makes you sustainable and increases your borrowing ability.

A big part of creating and sustaining wealth has come from being optimistic about my life. That has been a big part of my success. Without optimism, I wouldn't have my drive, and I probably would have settled for whatever money I made. *Optimism and drive have steered me away from complacency.*

Wise investments bring generational wealth. I think about my daughter and potential grandchildren. It's my responsibility to be a good steward of the wealth I've made. Part of making money is spending money, but you have to make good investments. Income-producing real estate is a good investment. Be a good steward of what you've made, as well. Save and invest.

I'm not generally a seller of real estate, although I do sell some. I've met so many wealthy real estate families, and most of them don't sell, which reminded me of when I played Monopoly as a kid. When I had Boardwalk and Park Place, I accumulated value and wealth because I didn't sell. Acquiring the right real estate on the board made me a winner, and it still does today.

I believe that with anything you do, you have to give it your all. It sounds cliché, but most people don't. Mediocrity is not acceptable, and it is not a winning strategy. If you don't want to give what you are currently doing your all, do something else and give that your all. When I discovered precisely what I loved doing and committed to making it my career, I gave it my all. When I transitioned to real estate development, it was innate. *I love it.* It's hard to believe that people aren't willing to do what they love, because happiness is something that money doesn't buy. But if you are giving something your all, and you are not seeing the results, do something else, as I have done.

The reason people don't do something else is fear. They are afraid that they cannot afford to make the change and fearful that it may not work out. It definitely won't work if they don't try.

Confidence is critical, and you will have it if you educate yourself. In anything that you decide to do, you have to believe in yourself. Figure out what you're good at and have an open mind when you are trying to ascertain what is best for you. People aren't willing to experiment and discover the best way to use their skill set because they are too quick to settle. Initially, it may have seemed as though I was taking on too many jobs. I was young and hungry for success. That was part of the process to discover who I was destined to become and what I was destined to do. I painted rocks, washed cars, washed windows, had a lawn mowing business, ran Chuck's Skate Shop, was the mouse at Chuck E. Cheese, did ductwork, was a gas station attendant, delivered papers, was a DJ, owned a teen club, owned a stucco and drywall company, started a vending machine business, flipped homes, built homes, and ultimately became the owner of a billion-dollar real estate development company—Unicorp National Developments.

Don't be afraid to create your own brand, like Facebook, Google, Instagram, and Amazon. We have created our own unique brand, which has set us apart from our competition. Do the unexpected and be confident in that!

Aside from the many jobs I've had, I've owned several other businesses. I own farm-to-table restaurant Slate, an executive mini-office suite, and a small cable company. I've developed the Orlando StarFlyer, the world's tallest swing ride, and I am currently rolling out a new hotel chain called ZEN; we've established the trademark meaning Zest, Energy, and Nirvana, which will be a spa-like hotel chain focused on health and wellness. At one point, I owned a helicopter business, which concluded the dream I had of one day owning the collection of models I put together as a kid and kept on my dresser and rebuilding the symbol of my broken relationship with my dad.

In *Perseverance: Broke to Billions,* I have shared my journey and where I came from. Once you achieve a level of success, you have to use that influence responsibly. Sharing inspirational stories provides the opportunity to reveal lessons and advice on how people can enrich their lives. Use your circumstances to challenge you to discover your destiny.

———

Although I didn't have a father in my life, I didn't use that as an excuse not to be a good and loving father to my beautiful daughter, Riley. It didn't prevent me from learning the things that I wished he had taught me, nor did it preclude me from being the best version of myself.

Once my parents divorced when I was twelve years old, I never saw or heard from my father again. He went on with his life, as did I, but time brought my father back to me. After he lost his battle with cancer and was buried without my knowledge, his widow sent a small package to my mother. When Mom opened it, she realized that the contents were for me. I went over to Mom's house and retrieved the package along with a handwritten note that read, "Chuck kept this on his desk." It was a blue rock that I had painted when I was a little boy. I painted that particular rock my favorite color and gave it to my father so he would think about me every time he saw it. And he did.

I removed the rock from the package, held it in the palm of my hand, and closed my eyes. It was as if I could feel my father holding it one last time. That blue rock was an affirmation that, after all of those decades, what I believed when I painted it was true. Things mean something to people, regardless of how big or small they are.

The similarity is that my daughter Riley made me a three-inch plastic heart out of beads that she ironed and melted together. She said, "Dad, when you travel, I want you to think of me." That little heart has been in my travel bag since Riley was eleven years old. The smallest things can make the greatest impact.

When you build or create something, do so with the expectation that it will have significance to someone. *Give it value.* Put your heart and passion into it and leave your imprint. What is to come, will come—happiness, respect, opportunity, and the byproduct of doing well is recognition and often money. In the meantime, have integrity, be patient, passionate, and work hard. When challenges arise, remain committed and focused, and find a way to persevere even in the darkest of times.

Afterword

It is not easy to build wealth or accomplish what you desire most without perseverance. Perseverance is when you encounter challenges and fight to find a way forward. Perseverance will help you build the life that you envision.

Although I faced a great deal of adversity, setbacks, and short-term failures, I sustained a mindset that helped me persevere through it all. I was always passionate, but not obstinate. In some situations, I knew when I had learned hard lessons and deemed it was time to walk away, but not from the knowledge that I gained. I took it with me and used it as I moved forward, optimistic about my life and future endeavors. Know when you are approaching that cliff, but don't quit the journey of discovering who you are; take the lesson and another route to your destiny.

Acknowledgments

First and foremost, I would like to thank my beautiful wife, Ronna, who has always been with me throughout this journey and supported me through the difficult times and celebrated the good times with me, too.

To my beautiful daughter and successor, Riley, who is dedicated to climbing the ropes that I have climbed and continuing the legacy of our great company.

To my team at Unicorp, my friends, and family who have given me support throughout the years.

I further acknowledge the people who made a difference in a child's life without realizing it: Boy Scout leader George Guth; the teachers who saw the greater good in me; the neighbors that gave me a chance to prove myself; the lenders that believed in me when the rest of the world wouldn't.

I truly acknowledge that getting ahead in life is not what you do for yourself. It's what you do for others and then how the world rewards you for your efforts and goodwill. Always remember the Golden Rule.

Lastly, I would like to acknowledge Marala Scott. She was the pen in my hand. Without her kindness and thoughtfulness,

Acknowledgments

I would not have been able to produce this wonderful book. She truly was an inspiration to my writing and was able to help me relive my past so I could share it with you, the reader. My hope is that our work together will help inspire others to realize that hard work and perseverance can lead to success.

About the Author

Chuck Whittall is the founder and president of Unicorp National Developments Inc.

Mr. Whittall came from modest beginnings. As a lifelong resident of Central Florida, he had an entrepreneurial spirit at a young age. At the age of twelve, Mr. Whittall started his own lawn mowing business and at eighteen opened a successful teenage nightclub. With a strong interest in construction, he pursued and received his Class A general contractor's license and formed a construction company that he owned and operated for several years before venturing into the world of real estate development.

In 1998, Mr. Whittall founded Unicorp National Developments Inc., which has designed and constructed numerous retail developments; over one hundred drugstores, town centers, and luxury apartment complexes; ICON Park in Orlando; and the world's tallest swing ride, the StarFlyer. His projects to date have an aggregate value of over $3 billion. With great poise and vision, Mr. Whittall has built a company with an outstanding team that is often recognized by the *Orlando Business Journal* and *Orlando Sentinel* as the premier development company in Central Florida.

Chuck has received numerous recognitions, including:

- Ernst & Young Entrepreneur of the Year—2019 Regional Award Winner in Florida
- American Heart Association's 2015 Dick Pope Legacy Award
- Game Changers of the Year 2013
- Noted as a top CEO in Central Florida 2014–2018
- 50 Most Powerful Businessmen in Central Florida 2014–2018
- Unicorp named one of the Top Privately Held Companies in *Orlando Sentinel*'s 2018 Top 100 Companies
- 2017 Structures Awards Developer of the Year

Having a philanthropic heart, Mr. Whittall has been involved with many charities and strongly believes in giving back to the community. He was appointed chairman of the American Heart Association of Central Florida for 2016–2017 and had a record-breaking year for the Orlando chapter, raising over $400,000 for this great cause. He was recognized as the organization's 2019 Legacy Honoree at the Heart Ball for his continued support and fundraising.

ChuckWhittall.com
Unicorp.com